The ESSENTIALS of

Canadian History

Pre-Colonization to 1867:
The Beginning of a Nation

Terry A. Crowley, Ph.D.
Professor, Department of History
University of Guelph
Guelph, Ontario

TRANSFERRED
TO YRDSB

Research & Education Association
61 Ethel Road West
Piscataway, New Jersey 08854

THE ESSENTIALS®
OF CANADIAN HISTORY
Pre-Colonization to 1867:
The Beginning of a Nation

Printed in the United States of America

Library of Congress Catalog Card Number 99-76348

International Standard Book Number 0-87891-916-3

ESSENTIALS is a registered trademark of
Research & Education Association, Piscataway, New Jersey 08854

What the "Essentials of History" Will Do for You

REA's "Essentials of History" series offers a new approach to the study of history that is different from what has been available previously. Each book in the series has been designed to steer a sensible middle course, by including neither too much nor too little information.

Compared with conventional history outlines, the "Essentials of History" offer far more detail, with fuller explanations and interpretations of historical events and developments. Compared with voluminous historical tomes and textbooks, the "Essentials of History" offer a far more concise, less ponderous overview of each of the periods they cover.

The "Essentials of History" are intended primarily to aid students in studying history, doing homework, writing papers and preparing for exams. The books are organized to provide quick access to information and explanations of the important events, dates, and persons of the period. The books can be used in conjunction with any text. They will save hours of study and preparation time while providing a firm grasp of and insight into the subject matter.

Instructors too will find the "Essentials of History" useful. The books can assist in reviewing or modifying course outlines. They also can assist with preparation of exams, as well as serve as efficient memory refreshers.

In sum, the "Essentials of History" will prove to be handy reference sources at all times.

The authors of the series are respected experts in their fields. They present clear, well-reasoned explanations and interpretations of the complex political, social, cultural, economic, and philosophical issues and developments that characterize each era.

In preparing these books REA has made every effort to ensure their accuracy and maximum usefulness. We are confident that each book will prove enjoyable and valuable to its user.

Dr. Max Fogiel, Program Director

Acknowledgment

We would like to thank Ab Carr of Morrisburg (Ontario) Public School for his editorial review of this book.

CONTENTS

CHAPTER 1

Commercial Outpost and Evangelical Mission

1.1   Aboriginal Peoples

Our knowledge of Canada prior to the arrival of the first Europeans is fragmented and open to contention. The generally accepted theory holds that North America's aboriginal peoples migrated from Asia across the Bering Strait. While the timing of these migrations is disputed, humans were present in the Americas between 15 000 and 10 000 B.C. They were a rich diversity of peoples whose lifestyles varied with each locality. They migrated within the continent. Inuit, for instance, occupied part of the north shore of the St. Lawrence River until driven farther north by Montagnais Indians, who called them *Eskimo* ("eaters of raw meat"*).

While the number of aboriginal peoples north of Mexico at the time of the Europeans' arrival has been estimated at 10 million, those in what is now Canada varied between a half million and two and a half million. Amer-Indians have been classified according to linguistic, tribal, and cultural traits, such as are described in the following.

The first Indians that Europeans met were the Eastern Woodland Indians. Basically, they are divided into two groupings, the Algonkian (or Algonquin) and Iroquoian speaking peoples. Algonkians such as the Beothuk in Newfoundland (who became extinct in the nineteenth century) and the Micmacs of the Maritimes, the Maliseets

---

*Today this designation is viewed in most quarters as inaccurate, and as a result, many Inuit regard *Eskimo* as derogatory. —Ed.

Settlements Among Aboriginal Peoples

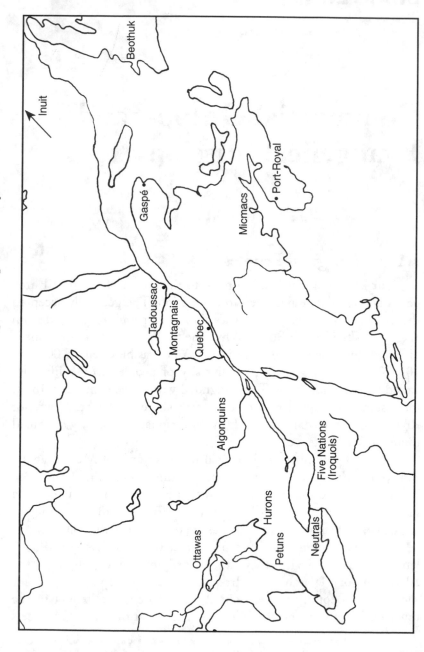

(Malecites) of New Brunswick, and the Montagnais, Ottawas, and Algonquins of central Canada were foragers who lived in small bands of 20 to 100 people and hunted and fished.

Iroquoian speaking peoples lived further inland and engaged in "slash and burn" agriculture. They included two important confederacies: the Huron, consisting of the Bear, Rock, Cord, and Deer peoples in the area between Lake Simcoe and Georgian Bay in Ontario; and the Iroquois or Five Nations, Six Nations after they were joined by the Tuscaroras in the early eighteenth century—the Mohawks, Senecas, Oneidas, Onondagas, and Cayuga, living principally south of Lake Ontario. The Petun, Erie, and Neutral nations in southwestern Ontario were other Iroquoians. This linguistic grouping of people lived in longhouses, containing 20 to 30 families, and settled in villages that moved every decade or so in search of fertile ground in which to grow maize and other vegetable crops.

Peoples living in the West and on the West coast had a different manner of food-gathering. Peoples living on the Plains used horses to hunt bison (buffalo), while others living in woodlands and parklands obtained food through different means. The Crees, who were Algonkian speakers, and Assiniboines were the largest groupings. The aboriginal peoples of the West coast lived off the wealth of the sea. Settled in villages with wooden buildings, they developed hierarchical societies divided into nobles, commoners, and slaves.

In the north, above the 56th parallel, various Athapaskan speakers hunted animals such as caribou and moose in small bands and fished, while in the Arctic, the Inuit ("the people") depended on sea mammals for their living.

1.2   European Background

While archaeology has shown that the Norse landed in Newfoundland at L'Anse-aux-Meadows—and it is generally agreed that Leif Ericsson reached mainland North America around A.D. 1000—continuous contact with Europe was not begun until fishermen began to fish off Canada's Atlantic coast in the late 1400s. French, English, Spanish, and Portuguese were soon involved.

Fishing did not require settlements. The Atlantic cod salted and preserved in barrels on board ships at sea was referred to as the "wet" or "green" fishery, while that cured on beach racks was called the "shore" or "dry" fishery. Only much later, when small settlements began, did distinctions develop between the inshore and deep sea fisheries. For over a century Canada functioned as a commercial "outpost" where fish were caught and furs traded with coastal Indians.

Intensive European involvement in Canada dated approximately from the creation of more centralized states in Europe, the development of better navigational tools, and competition spurred by Spanish and Portuguese interest in Mexico and South America. Most Europeans sought profits from the New World; a few searched for glory, particularly by discovering a route to the riches of Asia by sailing west; and others dreamed of making Christians of the new peoples encountered. While religious and humanitarian motives prompted a few settlements, the search for profits provided the primary motive.

1.3   Early Sojourners

King Henry VII of England commissioned Giovanni Caboto, an Italian, to search for a route to the East. In 1497, he landed at either Newfoundland or Cape Breton Island, claiming what he thought was part of Asia as an English possession. When Caboto disappeared during his second voyage in the following year—and King Henry VII died—English interest in a Northwest Passage lapsed temporarily. It was resumed by Martin Frobisher, who reached Baffin Island in 1576. John Hudson, sponsored by the Dutch, sailed through the body of water that bears his name today, Hudson's Bay, and went as far south as James Bay during his last voyage in 1610.

The Portuguese were great seafarers. In 1500 and 1501, Gaspar Corte-Real reached Newfoundland. João Alvares Fagundes explored the Gulf of St. Lawrence in 1520; and a Portuguese settlement was started on Cape Breton Island, but conflicts with aboriginal peoples led to its demise.

Fearful of Spanish expansion further to the south, King Francis I of France sent the Italian Giovanni da Verrazano, who explored the coasts (including Newfoundland) in 1524.

Jacques Cartier made three voyages in 1534, 1535, and 1541. During the second he reached Stadacona (Quebec City) and Hochelga

(Montreal). Conditions were difficult, and many men died from disease and malnutrition. Cartier returned to France with iron pyrite (fools' gold) and quartz crystals— hence the expression for something fake, *voilà un diamant du Canada* (that's a diamond from Canada).

Sir Humphrey Gilbert arrived at St. John's, Newfoundland in 1583 and claimed the island for Elizabeth I, but no permanent settlement was begun. Only fishing—and the trade in furs that grew from it—continued to attract Europeans. Each year 8-10 000 European fishers crossed the Atlantic.

A change in men's fashion late in the sixteenth century created demand for furs used to make wide-brimmed hats. "Greasy beaver" robes worn by the Indians were prized for their suppleness. When the robes were worn, the coarse outer hairs fell out and exposed the felt beneath. Unworn or dry beaver pelts were also sought. Each side, European and Indian, benefited in the trade. For the Europeans, profits were huge. Some amounted to 1400 percent.

1.4 First Attempts at Colonization and Evangelization

As more people rushed to secure furs, the French government decided to restore order by granting a monopoly over the trade. Attempts by monopoly holders to establish year-round bases on Sable Island in 1598 and elsewhere in 1600 ended in failure.

The British were more heavily involved in Newfoundland. The attempt by Sir George Calvert to establish a colony on Newfoundland in 1621 was unusual in being motivated by religion. A convert to Roman Catholicism, Calvert hoped to establish a haven where religious toleration would prevail. Fraught with internal discord between Protestants and Catholics, the settlement collapsed in 1629. But the Calvert family would later be more successful in bringing religious toleration to a new colony in Maryland.

In 1603, the Sieur de Monts obtained a 10-year monopoly of the Canadian fur trade on condition that he settle 60 colonists. Choosing the Bay of Fundy area, the group settled first on the Ste. Croix River and then moved across the bay to Port-Royal (present-day Annapolis Royal). It was a poor choice, as the furs obtained from the Indians were insufficient to cover costs. Champlain established the Order of

Good Cheer as a social club to lift spirits during a difficult winter. The first theatrical presentation, the *Théâtre de Neptune*, was mounted by poet and playwright Marc Lescarbot in 1606, but Port-Royal, however, was abandoned. In 1608, Samuel de Champlain established a new post at Quebec, where the St. Lawrence River narrows. The Europeans had gained a permanent foothold at last, but the primary goal remained commerce.

After Port-Royal was reoccupied by the French, the question of evangelization of the country's indigenous peoples came to the fore. The first baptisms of Micmac Indians by a Roman Catholic priest occurred in 1610. The rite was a sham as the priest did not know the Indians' language. Two Jesuits who arrived in Acadia the next year were horrified.

1.4.1 French Conform to Indian Alliances

At Quebec, Champlain directed the colony. As the Europeans were so few in number and the Indians tended to migrate, no immediate opposition was encountered. Champlain cemented the French position by forging alliances with the northern trading nations. He quickly identified the Hurons as essential to French fur trading, due to their role as middlemen in exchanges to the west and north. In 1609, he accompanied 60 Hurons and Algonkians down the Richelieu River to the lake now bearing his name. The crude guns of the French sent the Mohawks flying in the opening round of fighting—a conflict that would continue intermittently for nearly a century.

The French eventually established a full trading alliance with the Huron Confederacy. Their geographical location and maize-based economy made them intermediaries in the exchange of furs. In 1610 an 18-year-old Frenchman was sent to winter among the Hurons and five years later Champlain made his last wilderness alliance to cement the arrangement. By the 1620s, the Hurons were supplying one-half to two-thirds of the furs obtained by the French.

The prevailing economic idea, called mercantilism, held that colonies should supply the "mother" country with resources while consuming its manufactured products. To provide a larger population so that the French colonies in Canada might perform these functions better, Cardinal Richelieu created the *Company of One Hundred Associates* in 1627. In return for the fur-trade monopoly, the company was to send 200 colonists a year to Quebec. An important section in the charter limited migration to French Roman Catholics, thus ending earlier Protestant influence in the commercial companies. Some Protestants continued to come to New France, but they were subject to restrictions. Protestant religious services were not permitted. All office holders had to be Roman Catholics. Indians who professed the Catholic faith were to be treated as French nationals. The French thus recognized the rights of the aboriginal peoples individually, but did not consider them as nations with rights to land.

From the outset, the Company of One Hundred Associates was plagued with problems. The Kirke brothers, British pirates who had seized Port-Royal in 1627, captured the Associates' expedition in the following year. Quebec fell to them in 1629, although it was returned to France in 1632.

1.4.2 French/Indian Cultural Interaction

As there were never more than 100 French in Canada before 1630, cordial relations with Indian allies were essential. Europeans, nevertheless, had views about native peoples that were as strong as those the aboriginals had about the newcomers. Champlain, for instance, had hoped that conversion to Christianity would assimilate Indian allies to French ways. Catholic priests made little headway, nor did the Jesuits initially after they landed at Quebec in 1625. In fact, the French adapted to Indian ways more readily than vice versa. From the Indians, the French acquired the birch bark canoe, snowshoes, toboggans, moccasins, and food such as squash, beans, and corn.

While the Indian peoples varied greatly, they also shared some common characteristics. Marriage and divorce were easily obtained. Natives were horrified at French disciplinary methods with children. Social life remained highly consensual; community solidarity was more important than individual rights. Gift giving was important and Indians reproached the newcomers for their material selfishness. The indigenous peoples were less hierarchical than the Europeans. Their religions stressed the need for unity and harmony. Indians accepted French missionaries partially out of curiosity but largely because the newcomers were insistent.

Indians valued European goods, especially cooking utensils, cutting instruments, guns, and alcohol. Liquor became a major disruptive influence among most peoples. Champlain banned the trade in whisky, but to no avail. Competition from the Dutch established at Fort Orange (Albany) on the Hudson River, and later the English, conspired with the continent's vast extent to make such prohibitions meaningless.

1.5 Missionary Activity

After the Jesuits returned to Quebec in 1632, their attempt at assimilating Indian youth through education quickly proved a failure. They opened a regular school called the Jesuit College in 1635. Two years later the first reserve for Indians was opened to train Indians in agriculture, but it also ended in failure. These reserves would eventually surround Quebec's principal settlements and dot the Maritimes.

Jesuits and other orders ministered around the Atlantic coast. But that area was marked by feudal conflicts that inhibited colonization. The Jesuits decided to concentrate their efforts on the Huron confederacy despite its distance from Quebec. In 1639, the Jesuits established an impressive central mission at Ste. Marie (near Midland, Ontario) from which priests fanned out into surrounding villages. The Jesuits also appointed lay servants (*donnés*) who were sworn to their service and who, unlike the priests, could carry firearms.

1.5.1 The Jesuits and Their *Relations*

In the early seventeenth century, a new wave of religious fervour spread across France. This Catholic Counter-Reformation was in reaction to the birth of Protestantism. To tap this wellspring of faith and to garner support in France for their missions, the Jesuits published an annual account from 1632 to 1673 called the *Relations*. Their publications had two immediate consequences.

Marie de l'Incarnation and two other members of the Ursuline teaching order arrived at Quebec to teach Indian and French children in 1639. On the same ship came three Augustinian nuns from Dieppe who began an infirmary for Indians at Sillery in 1640 and later established the Quebec hospital, the Hôtel Dieu. They had responded to Jesuit pleas for assistance in the mission field.

Montreal, which would become Canada's largest city for more than a century, traces its roots to a mission inspired by the Jesuits'

Relations. The origins of the settlement, established in 1642, lay in France with a pious but secret religious group, the Company of the Holy Sacrament, which spawned a subsidiary under the name of the Society of Our Lady of Montreal for the Conversion of the Indians. Under the command of a career soldier, a small contingent established the mission of Ville-Marie. Although Montreal lived under constant Iroquois harassment and its population stagnated during the first decade, more settlers arrived as the mission became a fur-trading centre. Marguerite Bourgeoys arrived in 1653 and later established the largest teaching order in early Canada, the Sisters of the Congregation of Our Lady. Women were involved in the missionary enterprise to an unprecedented extent.

1.5.2   Success and Failure in Huronia

A series of disastrous epidemics followed the European invasion of the Americas, because indigenous peoples had no resistance to new diseases. The Hurons, previously more numerous than the Iroquois, saw their population halved to some 10 000 people between 1635 and 1640.

Conversions proceeded slowly as priests like Jean de Brébeuf learned the language, compiled dictionaries, and translated instructional materials. Up to 19 clergy ministered in the area at any one time. The numbers of adult Hurons baptized increased significantly after the founding of Ste. Marie.

Traditional enemies of the Hurons, the Iroquois increased their raids as furs in their own territories became depleted. With guns distributed by the Dutch and French, the severity of warfare increased.

Iroquois incursions into Huronia reached new heights in 1648, and the following year the Hurons were defeated. Survivors sought refuge on Christian Island in Georgian Bay and then found a permanent home in Quebec. Whether or not the Huron response to Iroquois attacks was weakened by divisions created by Christianity is debated by historians. Nonetheless, the Iroquois were unable to replace the Hurons as middlemen in the fur trade even though they dispersed the surrounding peoples.

1.6   Commercial Expansion

The monopoly of the Quebec trade was sublet to a group of resident merchants called the Communauté des Habitants in 1645. As more profits remained in Quebec, the basis for some individual fortunes was established, but this arrangement did not last long.

The French increasingly sought out new sources of furs in the interior. Individual traders were called *coureurs de bois* ("runners of the woods") and they frequently took Indian companions, creating a mixed blood population called métis. Later, the men handling the canoes were called *voyageurs*.

1.7   Seigneurial System

The seigneurial system was begun in Acadia and was extended to New France in 1627. Although feudal in origin and military in intent, the seigneurial system in Canada became a form of land holding intended to promote settlement. The Company of One Hundred Associates made grants of large tracts of land to other seigneurs or landed gentry. Seigneurs might be granted rights allowing them to dispense justice or to maintain a mill. In return, they had to swear loyalty to the king and provide a general plan and census of their seigneury. A tax had to be paid when a seigneury changed hands. Seigneurs were generally nobles. About a quarter of the land ceded under seigneurial tenure was given to various parts of the Roman Catholic Church.

While the seigneurial system provided for orderly land settlement, it rested on the concepts of paternalism and hierarchy. An annual token cash payment to the seigneur was required in addition to other yearly dues as rent for the land. The seigneur might also impose a *corvée* or compulsory days of work for the development of his personal land. As land was readily available and the standard of living was higher than in France, Quebec's farmers preferred to be called *habitants* (residents) rather than peasants as they would be labelled in Europe. While habitants did not own the land in the same way as in British freehold land tenure, the system of written contracts that developed ensured security of land holding.

1.8   Developments in Atlantic Canada

The Maritimes were a vast, separate colony called Acadia. Semi-feudal fighting between two French families came to an end in 1645. A governor was named and he was given a monopoly of the fur trade. Roman Catholic missionaries attempted to convert native peoples, but fishing and fur trading remained the principal activities.

Acadia was lost to the English in 1654 and not returned to France until 1667. France strengthened its position in relation to the North Atlantic fisheries by establishing a colony at Placentia in southern Newfoundland in 1662.

1.9   The Need for Reorganization

French settlement in Acadia remained so weak that the English took Port-Royal in 1654. A peace reached in the same year between the Iroquois and the French in the St. Lawrence valley did not prove lasting. Raids against French Canadian farmers and communities increased. By 1663 there were only some 3000 settlers in Quebec and no more than 500 in Acadia, but the English colonies to the south contained 100 000 people. While a continent was unfolding, the ideals for colonization expressed in the creation of the Company of One Hundred Associates had not been realized.

CHAPTER 2

Royal Government (1663-1689)

2.1 Royal Absolutism

The limited development of the French colonies in North America and the threats posed by the Iroquois led the French government to end company rule in Quebec (New France) in 1663 and in Acadia in 1670. Royal government remained in place until the end of the French regime in Canada.

New France and Acadia bore the strong imprint of the centralizing, bureaucratic institutions of the absolutist monarchy that emerged under Louis XIV. The key figure in bringing the transfer of these structures to North America was Jean-Baptiste Colbert, the king's chief minister who was also responsible for the navy and colonies.

Absolutism insisted on undivided sovereignty and no political opposition. Ideas about the divine right of kings underpinned absolutism. Rival authorities, such as the nobility and the clergy, were subordinated.

As a centralizing and bureaucratizing force, absolutism fostered the modernization of political institutions. Royal officials spread out around the kingdom to direct social, political, and economic life. They reported directly to the government ministries located at the royal court of Versailles, outside Paris. The centralism effected by the Bourbon monarchs put an end to the religious and civil wars that had racked France.

2.2 Mechanisms of Government

The foremost instruments of absolutism in government were the *intendants* responsible for justice, public order, civil administration, and finance. Below them stood an ordered hierarchy of officials responsible for the execution of policy. Intendants generally belonged to families who had acquired their nobility through government service ("nobility of the robe").

Traditional authority continued to be represented in the governor general, who resided at Quebec, and subordinate governors in other communities. They conducted foreign affairs and relations with the Indians. Drawn from the prestigious military nobility ("nobility of the sword"), they led the colonial regulars and militia.

Meritocratic bureaucracy and centralization were only partially achieved. Many government offices in France continued to be venal, i.e., they could be bought. Sometimes such purchases carried ennoblement. Agents of a few venal office holders held positions in the colonial administration, notably in finance. Status was very important. Nobles were not allowed to engage in retail trade without derogation, the loss of privileges they enjoyed.

Assemblies were not permitted without government approval. Collective petitions were also prohibited, although merchants in Montreal and Quebec were later allowed to elect representatives called syndics to express their views. The governor and intendant nevertheless authorized meetings for public consultations such as the "Brandy Parliament" of 1678, where fur traders were asked their views about the trade in whisky with the Indians.

Nevertheless, public protest occurred intermittently during the course of the French regime, often in response to high prices. Women were particularly noticeable during demonstrations in 1757 and 1758 that formed in response to the availability of bread. Government generally responded leniently to such protests, unless violence or damage to property had occurred.

As the colonies were too poor to support a printing press and as absolutism entailed government censorship, politics were internalized within administrative structures. Factions tended to polarize around the governor and intendant. Conflicts were frequent.

2.2.1 Administration of Justice

The nature of government in New France was revealed in its judicial system. An important part of royal government entailed the creation of a colonial high court, the Sovereign or Superior Council, which heard cases on appeal from lower courts. The court exercised both judicial and legislative functions.

Lawyers were banned from the colonies on the grounds that they created too much litigation. Notaries did legal paperwork. The Custom of Paris provided a set of legal precedents in civil matters that was augmented by judicial decisions and royal and local ordinances.

The legal system was inquisitorial rather than adversarial. There were no juries. Guilt was assumed until innocence was established by court-appointed officials investigating disputes. Torture might be employed in extraordinary circumstances, but was used sparingly. Penalties imposed were at the judge's discretion.

Despite these drawbacks, justice was remarkably swift and impartial. Serious crime such as robbery, murder, and rape was minimal.

2.3 Military Intervention

To establish conditions for growth, Colbert sent a regiment to Quebec in 1665. Consisting of 1000 soldiers, they marched into Mohawk country. The Mohawks sought a truce that brought an end to the wars waged intermittently since 1609. When the regiment returned to France, some soldiers chose to settle in Quebec.

2.3.1 Militia

Militia companies were organized in 1669 to augment colonial defences. All men from ages 16 to 60 were required to serve. Each militia unit was headed by a captain, but the *capitaines de milice* were not seigneurs. They were locally prominent individuals who served as intermediaries between the Crown and the people. The Canadian militia and the colonial regulars became experts in guerrilla warfare.

2.4 Immigration

Removing the Mohawk threat was critical to achieving growth in population. In the decade after 1666, more than 4000 immigrants were subsidized by the Crown to emigrate to New France. Many were soldiers and some 900 were young women drawn from orphanages and hospices. Since no similar program was initiated for Acadia, the European population of the Maritimes languished at 2000 inhabitants by 1707.

2.5 Population Policy

During the initial period of royal government, people were encouraged to marry young and to have many children. Parents with 10 or more children were rewarded with financial bonuses. Women who married under 16 years of age, and men under 20, received royal wedding dowries. Fathers whose children remained at home without marrying were fined.

Yet the population of New France continued to double every 20 to 25 years even after this program was abandoned. Rapid natural increase seems to have derived more from better food, plentiful fuel, and virtually free land.

2.6 Economic Program—Mercantilism

The French government was willing to invest in New France partially as a result of a prevailing economic idea called mercantilism. Since people believed that the world's wealth was limited, any state that increased its power and prosperity did so at the expense of another. Nations created colonies to consume home manufactures and to tap colonial natural resources.

2.6.1 The Colbert/Talon Program

The economic program formulated by Jean-Baptiste Colbert aimed at providing self-sufficiency in food, clothing, and shelter. Another goal was to diversify the economy through the establishment of tanneries, the expansion of fisheries, and the creation of a shipbuilding industry for intercolonial trade with the French West Indies.

Jean Talon, the first intendant in Canada (1665-72), supervised these initiatives but met with limited success. Ships could be built more cheaply in France: there were few craftspeople in the colony and labor was expensive. The Dutch and British were able to continue supplying the West Indies because their costs were much lower, even though such exchanges were theoretically illegal. Trade flowed naturally, as the thriving commerce between Acadia and New England showed. Enforcement of mercantilist regulations was too difficult and costly.

New France continued to rely on the export of beaver and Acadia on fishing. Even in the eighteenth century, furs constituted over 70 percent of the value of exports from Quebec. Attempts to tap the country's timber resources proved uneconomical.

The mercantilist policies were the least successful aspect of Colbert's plans for New France. Mercantilism promoted colonial trade while stunting other aspects of economic development.

2.7   The Role of the Roman Catholic Church

Since royal government and institutions such as the seigneurial system aimed at social control to avoid internal upheavals, the French monarchy also subsidized the Roman Catholic Church and allowed no other formal religious expression. The term gallicanism referred to the national rights of the French church, including the power of the king to nominate candidates for French bishoprics to the Pope. Ultramontanism described a papal alternative less trammelled by secular intervention.

The arrival of Sulpician priests at Montreal in 1657 and Quebec's first bishop, François de Laval, shortly after were important events that ended the Jesuit monopoly over priestly functions. In 1663, the Sulpicians became the seigneurs of Montreal. The state subsidized the church to allow it to operate hospitals, asylums, and schools.

The church was divided into a variety of men and women's religious orders. To train a Canadian clergy, Bishop Laval established two seminaries. With the infusion of new immigrants at the same time, the mystical practices seen previously among some of the colony's religious men and women began to wane.

To support a parish clergy Bishop Laval attempted to obtain an obligatory annual payment to the church called the *tithe*. Originally pegged at one-thirteenth of the value of the produce of the land, objections from the colonists led to government intervention that eventually reduced the amount.

New France suffered from a shortage of priests. With fewer than 200 male clergy by the end of the French regime for a population of approximately 75 000 people, many rural residents did not have regular access to religious services.

While the structures of the church were as hierarchical and authoritarian as those of the state, Canadians were much more independent compared to their counterparts in France. Neither church nor state was ever able to wield complete power due to competing authorities and the dispersion of Canadian settlements. The church as a whole, however, owned a significant number of seigneuries and was the largest single landowner.

2.8 Expansion West, North, and South

Geographical expansion remained inherent to the fur trading and missionary enterprises. New sources of furs were constantly sought, new peoples to evangelize, and the elusive route to Asia remained a dream. The fur traders Pierre-Esprit Radisson and his brother-in-law Des Groseilliers discovered the upper Mississippi, explored Lake Superior, and reached Hudson's Bay between 1658 and 1662.

Royal government brought greater state control over the organization and regulation of such expeditions. Jean Talon originated the plan for the explorations of Louis Jolliet and the Jesuit Jacques Marquette in hopes of finding a way to Asia. In 1673 Jolliet and Marquette travelled down the Mississippi as far as the present boundary between Arkansas and Louisiana. Cavelier de La Salle formally claimed the region extending to the Gulf of Mexico for France in 1682. He was intimately associated with Governor Frontenac (1672-81, 1689-98) in fur trading ventures, illustrating the close association between official position and personal profit-making.

2.9 Hudson's Bay

The English had discovered Hudson's Bay in 1610 and they remained the only Europeans to visit the area initially. With the assistance of Groseilliers and Radisson, they organized the Hudson's Bay Company in England in 1670 to pursue fur trading through the northern route.

While French explorers also moved northward from the St. Lawrence to meet the new competition, in 1686 an expedition that included Pierre Le Moyne d'Iberville captured the English forts at Moosonee, Rupert, and Albany.

2.10 The Nature of Colonial Society

The relative weakness or small size of the French colonies in comparison to those of the British continues to be debated.

Immigration into New France was different from that into New England, which had consisted of massive group migration for religious reasons. The French who settled in Canada came as individuals and families from diverse regions of a much larger country. Local customs and dialects broke down more quickly in Canada. Government subsidization of migration ended in the 1670s.

While there were fewer women than men in the French colonies, and while perhaps as many as 20 percent of Canadian males were involved in the western fur trade, no fundamental transformation of women's traditional roles took place. The legal code, *Coutume de Paris*, provided some limited protection of women's property rights; and the rights of widows were recognized by law and custom. On average, women married at the age of 22 and bore seven children. The Quebec population doubled every 25 years, and the Acadian population rose even more spectacularly in the eighteenth century.

Three-quarters of the population of New France lived within concessions strung out around waterways, which were the principal means of communication. Settlement in Acadia was dispersed around the Bay of Fundy. Many farmers participated in fur trading expeditions.

In comparison to French peasants, Canadian habitants lived easily, but in absolute terms they were poor. With the exception of occasional levies imposed for special purposes, the only taxes Canadians paid were those on the export of furs and the import of wine and liquor. In addition to seigneurial *corvées*, the Crown might also impose compulsory labor for public works such as the construction of fortifications. The tithe paid was small, but seigneurial rents amounted to a significant proportion of income. In European terms, French Canadian farmers were peasants, although they rejected that term.

Because immigrants to the French colonies came from many of France's diverse regions, language usage was initially very mixed, but Parisian French came to predominate. A rich heritage of song, dance, and music developed among the common people, although the church emerged as a major corporate patron of the arts.

The authoritarian apparatus of government and religion was not transferred to the countryside successfully. Many seigneurs were absentee landlords. The clergy of New France, never numerous, were concentrated in the towns. While an aristocratic ethos percolated down from the top of society, more egalitarian values permeated up from frequent interaction with Indian peoples. The French Canadian population became known for its independence and its status consciousness. Fine clothes and ownership of horses were marks of relative prosperity.

2.11 The Colonial Economy

The relative weakness of the early Canadian economy could be seen in continued dependence on fur exports from central Canada and fish from the Atlantic coast. These traits may be attributed to a variety of factors.

Societal values clearly distinguished the clergy, nobles, and business people (*bourgeoisie*), and others served to make the transition from passive consumption to larger career aspirations more difficult.

The military establishment grew in size and influence. Dominated by officers who were frequently nobles, the military came to consume resources that might otherwise have been applied to economic development.

Religious differences are the most difficult to pin down. The stress that Protestantism in the British colonies placed on the lone individual saved by faith alone through God's grace contrasted with the emphasis placed by Roman Catholicism on observance of the sacraments and the importance of good works in insuring salvation.

The lack of viable markets worked against early Canada. This resulted partially from its geographical location, although some agricultural surpluses were exported. Labor was scarce and the number of craftspeople was small.

Once the monopoly of the fur trade with France passed to the

Company of the West Indies in 1664, profits generally flowed in the direction of the "mother" country rather than remaining in the colony. Capital for economic diversification was lacking.

CHAPTER 3

Conflict of Empires (1689-1763)

3.1 Imperialism and Colonial Wars

As the colonies grew and as the old antagonisms between France and England erupted in more frequent wars, the scale of conflicts increased in North America. Beginning in the late seventeenth century, naval conflict became increasingly important. Warfare involving the French colonists and the Indians had consisted generally of small raids and guerrilla tactics. The results for both Acadia and Canada would be calamitous during the middle of the eighteenth century.

The rivalry between France and England originated in political, economic, and religious differences. While both countries were monarchies, the former was Roman Catholic and absolutist, the latter Protestant and parliamentary. While their foreign policies in regard to Europe brought the two into conflict, both also sought economic advantage through preying on enemy commerce during periods of conflict.

Wars declared in Europe were experienced with increasing effect in the colonies, but the names they acquired in Canada and Europe differed from those in the British colonies to the south. At such times, coastal settlements were more prone to attack than was, for instance, Quebec, because the treacherous waters of the St. Lawrence River made access more difficult. Port-Royal in Acadia and Placentia and St. John's in Newfoundland provided excellent refuges from which pirates swooped down on enemy ships to acquire booty during war.

By the mid-eighteenth century, antagonisms between the French and English colonies had reached such a stage that hostilities erupted in North America before France or England had declared war.

3.2 Transition to Settlement in Newfoundland

British settlement in Newfoundland grew slowly over the seventeenth century with immigrants coming principally from the West Country counties of Dorset, Devon, and Cornwell in England. West Country merchants believed settlement would lessen the profitability of their fishing enterprises, and the British government refused to establish a year-round governor in Newfoundland until 1729. Instead, the first fishing captain to arrive in port acted as admiral to settle disputes and to allot drying spaces during the fishing season.

In the eighteenth century, when the wintering population of the island had increased to some 7000 by 1753, the Irish outnumbered the English. They were principally Roman Catholics from southern Ireland, particularly the counties of Wexford and Cork. English ships began to abandon the inshore fishery in favour of the offshore banks, but overfishing had dried up stocks by mid-century. Labour saving techniques were implemented in offshore fishing operations and inshore fishers sought to diversify into salmon, furs, and seals, or moved to more northerly ports.

3.3 War of the League of Augsburg (King William's War) — 1689-1697

After England had formed a defensive alliance with Holland known as the League of Augsburg, war with France began in 1689. Massachusetts adventurer William Phips set out early that year to attack Acadian settlements and captured Port-Royal. In Quebec, Governor Frontenac mounted retaliatory raids on British settlements to force them to abandon their alliance with the Iroquois. The French also attacked St. John's in Newfoundland.

The Canadian born naval captain Pierre Le Moyne d'Iberville attacked St. John's in Newfoundland in 1694 and then proceeded north where he captured Fort York, the Hudson's Bay Company's trading post. During Iroquois attacks on the St. Lawrence settlements, a number of civilians distinguished themselves, including Madeleine de Verchères. The Canadian French attacked Onondaga and Oneida villages south of Lake Ontario.

The Treaty of Ryswick ended the war in 1697.

3.4   Peace with the Iroquois, 1701

As a result of growing conflicts, over 1000 Indians representing 32 nations met at Montreal to discuss future relations with the French. By the Treaty of Montreal in 1701, the French recognized the Iroquois as an independent nation and the Iroquois promised to remain neutral in any war between France and Britain.

3.5   Louisiana

In 1689, Pierre Le Moyne d'Iberville was dispatched to the mouth of the Mississippi River by the government of France to lay claim to the area north of the Gulf of Mexico. He returned in 1701 to establish a colony named Louisiana. In 1718, New Orleans was established. Louisiana was singularly unpopular in its early years due to lack of economic viability and disease. Felons, prostitutes, foreigners, and Protestants were sent for a brief period, but death rates for whites and slaves were high. Eventually the colony began to produce pitch, tar, furs, hides, silk, indigo, rice, and cotton for export. Jesuit, Capuchin, Carmelite, and Ursuline orders served religious, educational, medical, and social service needs.

The French were now increasingly able to see their colonies encircling the British colonies hemmed in along the coast by the Appalachian mountain range. As conflicts grew, fur-trading posts were manned by troops, and military considerations assumed a higher priority than economic activity.

3.5.1   Extension of the Fur Trade

The fur trade expanded in the Canadian West as well. In 1690-91, the first European reached the plains of Saskatchewan. By the 1730s, La Vérendrye and his sons had established fur-trading posts stretching from the western end of Lake Superior to Lake Winnipegosis. Alliances were made with a wide range of Indian tribes.

3.6　War of the Spanish Succession (Queen Anne's War)—1702-1713

The desire of Louis XIV to place a member of his dynasty on the throne of Spain led to another war in 1702. The French Canadian militia and their native allies conducted raids on British settlements in 1703 and 1704. British colonists assaulted Acadia for three years before capturing Port-Royal for the last time in 1710, changing its name to Annapolis Royal.

3.6.1　Treaty of Utrecht, 1713

The Treaty of Utrecht that ended the war marked a major retreat for France. Louis XIV agreed to cede Newfoundland, Nova Scotia (the name they now gave to their new colony), and Hudson's Bay to Britain. And he agreed to recognize formal British influence over the Iroquois. The French retained rights to Cape Breton and Prince Edward Island and the right to disembark in Newfoundland to dry their fishing catches along the northern coast (the "French Shore").

3.7　Acadia

While Acadians were allowed to repair to Cape Breton, which the French called Ile Royale, few chose to do so. French Roman Catholic missionaries continued to minister to Acadians' religious needs and to those of the Micmacs and Malecites who were firm allies of the French. The latter joined with Abenakis in Maine to resist British encroachment on their lands during a war from 1722-25. In the peace reached in 1725, the British promised not to interfere in Indian territory and the natives acknowledged King George as the "possessor of the province."

The Acadians, whose ancestors had come from southwestern France, lived on small farms that produced livestock for export to the British colonies. As their population expanded even faster than that in Quebec, British authorities worried about their loyalty and wanted them to swear an oath of allegiance. In 1730 a number of Acadians made such an oath after being assured that they would be exempt from military service and that their religion and property would remain undisturbed. The Acadians became known as the "Neutral French."

3.7.1 Louisbourg

In 1713 France consolidated its presence in the North Atlantic by establishing Louisbourg on Cape Breton Island. Louisbourg became the most massive fortress in North America—a walled city. As a base for French fishing activities and as a trans-shipment point for ships arriving from Canada, the West Indies, and the mother country, Louisbourg emerged as the first port in New France.

At the opening of the war of the Austrian Succession (King George's War, 1744-48), the large garrison at Louisbourg attacked the fishing settlement at Canso in Nova Scotia and Annapolis Royal. In retaliation, the British captured Louisbourg in 1745. By the Treaty of Aix-la-Chapelle three years later, Louisbourg was returned to France in exchange for other French conquests.

3.7.2 European Settlement on Prince Edward Island

This Gulf of St. Lawrence Island (which the French called Ile-Saint-Jean) was home only to Micmacs for part of each year until after the founding of Louisbourg. In 1720 the island was accorded to the Count of St. Pierre, a French nobleman. Six years later, the stationing of a French garrison symbolized the continuing European presence. Acadians began to migrate to the colony and engaged in farming and fishing.

3.8 Economy and Society During the French Regime

The French presence in North America was spread out. Canada proved unattractive to French emigrants due to its cold climate, limited opportunities, and frequent conflicts. Despite rapid natural increases, Quebec's population amounted to only 60 000 people by 1760.

The economy of Quebec remained heavily dependent on fur exports. While most people farmed, some 20-25 percent of men in the St. Lawrence valley were probably involved in the western fur trade at some point in their lives. Mercantilist policies prevented weavers from being sent to the colony after 1703 for fear that colonial production might detract from that in France. Yet the French government provided support for colonial ironworks and for—

uneconomical—shipbuilding. Sometimes small agricultural surpluses were exported, but crops were subject to draughts, disease, and insect infestations. Attempts to export timber proved unsuccessful because Canada could not compete with the Baltic states.

As Quebec frequently experienced trade imbalances, hard currency ("specie") was in such short supply that beginning in 1685 a colonial currency was developed. Playing cards signed by the indendant circulated as promissory notes, augmented after 1735 by military *ordonnance* (orders) that functioned in the same fashion. Canada, Louisiana, and Louisbourg remained heavily dependent on government expenditures, particularly military.

At the top of the social structure of early Canada stood the nobility, a class consisting of military officers, office holders, the highest church authorities, and some seigneurs. The prevalence of aristocratic values meant that society was divided not only along economic lines. Social rank dictated much economic behaviour. Keeping up appearances kept some of the colonial nobility in dire economic straits, although social distinctions based on rank were pronounced.

Merchants and entrepreneurs, both Protestant and Catholic, constituted a limited middle class. Below them were craftspeople and artisans.

Three-quarters of the people were peasant farmers whose homes were strung out along the waterways. The habitants were better off than their counterparts in France, but illiteracy was higher. Absenteeism among seigneurs was so common that the royal Edicts of Marly in 1711 threatened to revoke undeveloped seigneurial grants and tenant concessions. Excessive subdivision of landholding began to emerge after the third generation of settlement.

Social rituals included the *charivari* (shivaree), or mock serenade of a newly married couple that might assume menacing tones if the marriage challenged traditional norms. Men below the age of 30 and women below 25 belonged to their fathers and required their permission to marry. Common law relationships were frequent, especially among those venturing into the fur trade. Métis populations thus developed. Death in childbirth was relatively common among women and infant mortality high. About one in four children died during their first year. While the state came to assume responsibility for foundlings, some 80 percent of infants lodged by the Grey nuns at their Montreal hospice died, a mortality rate partially attributable to careless practices among the wet nurses to whom they were entrusted.

Families rather than individuals constituted the basic units in society. Marriage frequently cemented a family alliance or constituted a business arrangement. Women brought dowries in return for their husbands' patronage, but marriage contracts might provide dower rights to protect the wife's material interest in the marriage if her husband predeceased her. The average age for a woman to marry in New France (22) was lower than in France, but the younger ages at which people died shortened the length of marriages. A woman who survived her childbearing years in eighteenth-century Quebec might expect to bear seven or eight children, or even a higher number in Acadia.

About 4000 slaves lived in Quebec up to 1800. The French accepted the native practice of enemy enslavement; thus, more than half were aboriginals. Slaves, especially those of African descent, were so expensive that they were a mark of social prestige for the owner. Most were baptized in the Roman Catholic faith. Life expectancy was low—18 years for Indians and 25 for African-Canadians, as compared to nearly 50 for white colonials.

3.9   British Settlement in Nova Scotia

After the Treaty of Aix-la-Chapelle, the British decided to shore up their weak position in Nova Scotia. Halifax was established in 1749 as a naval base and as a settlement to counterpoise Louisbourg. Over 2500 people left England for the colony in 1749, many of them Irish.

A new source of immigrants was then sought among the "Foreign Protestants," mostly Swiss, French Huguenots, and Germans. As their presence proved disruptive, active recruitment was halted in 1752.

French and Spanish Territories, 1760

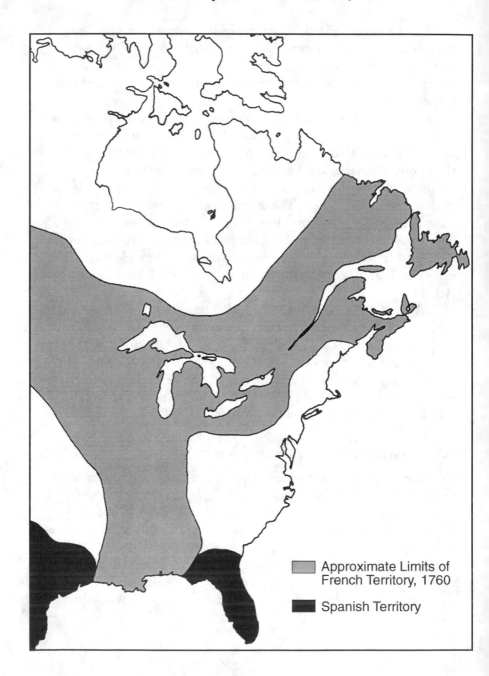

Approximate Limits of French Territory, 1760

Spanish Territory

3.10   The Seven Years' War (French and Indian War) — 1756-1763

Two years before war between France and Britain resumed in 1756, armed conflict between the two nations erupted in the Ohio River Valley and Nova Scotia.

3.10.1   Conflict in the Ohio Valley

The French government resolved to drive away the British who had found their way into the Ohio Valley. To protect Canada's southern flank, garrisons were strengthened. In 1753, the governor of Virginia dispatched George Washington to check the French, but the following year he was defeated. As a result, France and Britain sent army regiments to North America in 1755.

3.10.2   Deportation of the Acadians

Nova Scotia emerged as another place for international friction. The French attacks from Louisbourg during the War of the Austrian Succession had again raised the question of Acadian loyalty to Britain.

The French constructed Fort Beauséjour on the Isthmus of Chignecto, near the present border with New Brunswick. In 1755 the British attacked and captured Beauséjour. Unfortunately, some 200 Acadians were found within the walls of the fort.

Governor Charles Lawrence of Nova Scotia resolved to settle the loyalty issue. The alternatives he presented Acadian representatives consisted of either an unqualified oath or deportation. When the Acadians equivocated, Lawrence and his council carried through on his threat. In the years between 1755 and 1761, the majority of Acadians were rounded up from Nova Scotia (and later from Cape Breton and Prince Edward Island), allowed to carry only moveable belongings, and deported. While those who found their way to Massachusetts were treated fairly, colonies from New York to South Carolina proved more hostile. Some Acadians wandered into Louisiana (where their descendants, the Cajuns, still live), while others ended up in the French West Indies, France, or returned eventually to Canada. A sad page in Canadian history, the deportation of the Acadians was a military decision undertaken by local officials.

Nova Scotia was granted an assembly in 1758 and Governor Lawrence took advantage of a substantial British subsidy for the colony to subsidize the immigration of American settlers, the "New England Planters," between 1759 and 1762. About 8000 arrived, mostly farmers who occupied the former Acadian lands, and fishermen. Not finding conditions as good as expected, about half of the Planters left Nova Scotia.

3.10.3 The Fall of New France

Despite reverses in Nova Scotia and the great differences in the populations of the French and British colonies, the Seven Years' War initially went well for France. The French successfully defended approaches to New France via the Great Lakes and the Richelieu River.

Fortunes began to alter after William Pitt, who came to power in Britain in 1757, decided to commit greater resources to the North American theatre of war. The result was seen in the large-scale British attack and conquest of Louisbourg in 1758. The army under General Jeffrey Amherst and the navy commanded by Admiral Edward Boscawen reduced the fortress a second time. Louisbourg was eventually blown up to prevent the French from returning. Prince Edward Island surrendered and its Acadians were deported.

The British used Louisbourg as the launching pad for the assault on the town of Quebec in 1759. The town experienced severe difficulties, food shortages, and typhus.

The British spent months on the St. Lawrence River without being able to land near enough to the town. Under the command of General James Wolfe, the British were able to land just upriver from the capital and to scale the heights to the Plains of Abraham. The French General, Montcalm, foolishly ordered his troops out in European battle formation to meet the invaders. The French were defeated but Wolfe himself lay mortally wounded. The town surrendered shortly afterwards.

The French forces regrouped, under the Chévalier de Lévis, and returned to drive back the British at the Battle of Sainte Foy in 1760. The new British commander, General James Murray, repeated Montcalm's error and ended up routed as well. Only the later arrival of British naval vessels tipped the scales in favour of British forces under Jeffrey Amherst, who captured Montreal in 1760. The Montreal articles of capitulation granted freedom of worship and security of property, but no guarantees were given to the male Roman Catholic religious orders.

CHAPTER 4

The Early British Regime (1760-1791)

4.1 The British and the Indians

The peace reached in the Treaty of Paris (1763) secured Canada's fate as a British possession. France retained only the tiny islands of Saint Pierre and Miquelon off Newfoundland's southern coast, and surrendered her claims to lands east of the Mississippi. The part of Louisiana lying to the west was transferred to Spain in recognition of the latter's alliance with France during the Seven Years' War.

The British continued with their policy of forming alliances with native peoples through formal treaties, and in 1755 they established an Indian Department to provide greater coordination. They also decided that lands should be set aside for sole use by the aboriginal peoples.

Following treaties with the Malecites in 1760 and the Micmacs in the following year, Lieutenant-Governor Jonathan Belcher of Nova Scotia issued a proclamation ordering the removal of people settled on native lands and reserving the northeastern coast from the Musquodoboit River to the Baie des Chaleurs as Micmac hunting grounds.

Bitter over the defeat of their French allies, the Ottawa chief Pontiac organized a pan-Indian confederacy. William Johnson, the superintendent of northern Indians, urged a return to the gift diplomacy that had characterized earlier years, but General Amherst disagreed. In 1763 Indians attacked British forts in the upper Mississippi and Ohio River basins. At Fort Pitt the British military distributed smallpox infested blankets to the Indians. By 1764 Pontiac's confederacy dissolved. But the uprising had impressed upon the British the need for caution in relations with the continent's aboriginal peoples.

4.2   The Conquest and Quebec

From 1760 to 1764 Quebec was ruled under martial law. Soldiers, nonetheless, were kept in close check in their dealings with the civilian population. Between two and three thousand people returned to France rather than live under British rule. Various English-speaking merchants accompanied the army to Quebec. Although their numbers grew, there were fewer than a thousand English subjects in Quebec during the decade following the conquest. But they had the connections and capital to replace many of their French Canadian rivals. As mercantilism required that trade now be conducted only with the British, the Canadians' contacts in France were of little value. Many merchants faced bankruptcy because the paper orders that the French had substituted for currency during the war became increasingly worthless.

The French Canadians faced other difficulties, as Roman Catholics could not hold public office in Britain. As well, with the death of Quebec's bishop in 1760, the French Canadian church was left without an official to ordain new priests.

4.3   The Royal Proclamation, 1763

Britain's initial policy towards Canada was announced in the form of a royal decree in 1763—directed particularly towards Indians. The boundaries of Quebec were restricted and the interior of the continent west of the Allegheny mountains was set aside as a huge reserve for native peoples. Individuals were forbidden from purchasing these lands except through the British Crown at public meetings. Trade relations with the Indian nations were to be controlled strictly from London.

The Royal Proclamation also provided for four new colonial governments, including that at Quebec, to be ruled by British law.

4.4   Actions of the Early Governors

Strict enforcement of the Royal Proclamation would have out-lawed French Canadian civil law in Quebec and allowed British subjects to dominate an elected assembly, although British legal officials did announce that Roman Catholics in conquered territories were not subject to the same liabilities imposed in Britain.

Quebec's first two British governors, James Murray and Guy Carleton, were military men from aristocratic backgrounds who sympathized with the French Canadian elites rather than with merchants of their own ethnic background. The imposition of British common law in the colony created such disorder that Murray waived laws disqualifying Roman Catholics from serving on juries and being barristers. When Murray refused to call an assembly, the Anglophone merchants were so enraged that they secured his recall to England in 1766.

Guy Carleton followed Murray's views, particularly as he became increasingly concerned about ensuring the province's loyalty in the face of the increasing turmoil in the colonies to the south. In order to bond the Roman Catholic Church and the French Canadian seigneurs to Britain, the new governor sought to modify British policies.

4.5   The Quebec Act, 1774

As the policy of controlling the western fur trade from London had proven a failure, Quebec's ancient boundaries were restored by the Quebec Act in 1774 to allow more effective regulation out of the Canadian colony. Roman Catholics were allowed the free exercise of their religion—including the collection of the tithe by the church—but Jesuits were not allowed to recruit new members. French Canadian civil law was recognized, but English criminal law was continued. While these provisions pleased both seigneurs and church officials, English merchants were upset, especially as the Quebec Act also denied the assembly through which they hoped to influence the colony's public affairs. An appointive legislative council was created that could make laws with the governor's assent.

While the Quebec Act provided the means through which Carleton was able to co-opt Quebec's clergy and seigneurs, the secret instructions sent to the governor revealed that Britain was not yet prepared to be as lenient as the legislation appeared. Carleton was ordered to weigh the possibility of introducing English common law gradually, to survey the conduct of the bishop, and to regulate religious seminaries. The male religious communities were also to disappear, with the Jesuit order suppressed and its holdings confiscated. Carleton largely ignored these instructions, but the Jesuits were not allowed to recruit new members and their order eventually disappeared from Canada for a time.

4.6   Prince Edward Island

In 1767, the British had granted most of the island's townships to favourites of the king. Like the seigneurs in New France, the proprietors were to provide a conservative social structure and, more importantly, assume the costs of settling the island at their own expense. In 1769, the island became a separate colony with its own governor and the capital named Charlottetown in honour of the queen. Early settlers were heavily Scots, with the first landing in 1770, but tenants from Ulster arrived and London Quakers also established a base. Prince Edward Island's first Assembly was elected in 1773, but when many of the proprietors failed to live up to their responsibilities, the land question vexed the colony for a century.

4.7   The American Revolution

In 1775, the Second Continental Congress authorized George Washington to invade Quebec to forestall a British attack from the north. General Richard Montgomery led an American force through the Lake Champlain-Richelieu River route, captured Saint-Jean, and proceeded to Montreal. Carleton awaited the invading Americans in Montreal, but as half of his troops had been sent to help quell disturbances in Boston, he chose to flee to Quebec City to mount his defence. Montreal capitulated without fighting.

Worse, Carleton found that the mass of people were not prepared to follow those he had assumed to be their leaders. Seigneurs sent to enlist militia encountered extreme difficulties because farmers had enjoyed a decade and a half without compulsory military service.

Bishop Briand issued a circular telling people not to be seduced by American propaganda about liberty and he also threatened to withhold sacraments from any who rebelled.

A second American army led by Benedict Arnold reached the St. Lawrence. Joining Montgomery's forces, they laid seige to Quebec late in 1775. The cold winter and the town's natural defences worked to the advantage of the defenders, but again it was the arrival of the British navy in 1776 that forced the Americans to retreat south.

Frequent attacks by American privateers on coastal settlements alienated many people and caused severe food shortages in Newfoundland. In 1777, the British navy moved into the Bay of Fundy to ensure the area's loyalty.

No more than the French Canadians did the eastern Indians want to become entangled in this civil war. The neutrality of the Micmacs and Malecites was secured easily, but the Six Nations divided. Largely through the efforts of Joseph Brant, whose sister Molly Brant was companion to Indian superintendent William Johnson, the Mohawks and some of the Senecas supported the British. The Oneidas and Tuscaroras sided with the Americans, while other tribes remained neutral.

Joseph Brant gathered a force of Indians and settlers that was active in scouting and guerrilla attacks. His band joined Butler's Rangers (largely Senecas) in raids in the Mohawk Valley in 1778. The following year the Americans responded when General John Sullivan was ordered by Washington to lay waste to the countryside.

4.7.1 Henry Alline and the "New Light"

In Nova Scotia, where most of the New Englanders belong to the Congregational church, a religious revival called the Great Awakening occurred. Henry Alline disagreed with the Puritan emphasis on a strict rather than a loving God and on the preordained election of saints. Alline became an itinerant preacher who secured many converts to his Christian message of the "New Light" between 1776 and 1784.

4.8   The Loyalists in the Maritimes and Quebec

While the American Revolutionary War ended with the Treaty of Paris in 1783, loyalists to the British cause were not confined to geographical regions. The Royalists or Tories—as the Americans called them—were strongest in New York and weakest in Connecticut, Massachusetts, and Virginia. Many chose to depart. The British offered land, provisions, and building materials to assist relocation. Historians estimate the number coming into British North America at 50 000.

The Loyalists who came north were a heterogeneous group of men, women, and children. About half were civilians. Some were American born, but others came from Scottish, Irish, and German backgrounds. Huguenots and Quakers were counted among their numbers. Perhaps as many as 10 percent were of African descent, as the British had promised freedom to slaves who remained loyal to colonial governments. Some 2000 Loyalists were Indians.

The largest groups of Loyalists settled in the Bay of Fundy region, particularly around St. John, and in Nova Scotia. About 40 percent of Nova Scotia's Loyalists came from New York and a quarter from the southern colonies. While Shelburne was chosen for its immense harbour, the land in the immediate vicinity was not good for farming and the community declined after experiencing many difficult years.

Those of African descent had been promised not only freedom from slavery but also land. Unfortunately, the severe racial prejudice they encountered in Nova Scotia meant that far fewer blacks than whites secured land grants. About half of the black Loyalists departed in 1792 for Sierra Leone in Africa.

The Loyalists moving to Prince Edward Island also encountered disappointment. Proprietors reneged on giving them title to land. Many Loyalists left.

A much smaller number of Loyalists moved to Quebec, perhaps about 10 000. The majority were farmers from New York and Pennsylvania. Deciding that it would be unwise to settle the immigrants among the French Canadians, the governor arranged treaties with the Indians occupying southern Ontario. The purchases were completed by 1788.

Although the treaty by which Britain recognized the independence of the United States failed to mention the Indians, Iroquois Loyalists were provided two large land grants in Ontario. Joseph Brant and his group of Mohawks, Cayugas, and Onondagas chose the Grand River valley, while some hundred Mohawks followed John Deseronto to a tract of land in the Quinte region. The British also provided the Iroquois with other amenities, but disputes arose when the Grand River group began to sell off part of its holdings.

4.8.1 The Impact of the Loyalists

Loyalist migration ended by 1786 when compensatory land grants and provisioning virtually ceased.

The Loyalists were the single largest immigrant group that the northern colonies had absorbed. They brought with them a desire for freehold land tenure, English common law, and representative government. Those in the St. John River valley petitioned for their own government, which the British agreed to in creating New Brunswick in 1784. Its capital became Fredericton, named after one of the sons of George III. Loyalists in Ontario would have to wait until 1791 for their own separate colony.

As many of the Loyalists settling in the Maritimes were shop-keepers and artisans, a struggle developed between those who sought to import aristocratic political thought based on land holding and those from these ranks who were more committed to American democratic values. In 1787 Charles Inglis, a former Loyalist polemicist, arrived in Halifax as the first overseas Anglican bishop in the British empire. While most Loyalists were not Anglicans, Inglis tried to enhance the position of England's confessional church and he supported the founding of King's College in Windsor, Nova Scotia. Loyalists were also instrumental in founding the Provincial Academy of Arts and Science, which received its charter as the College of New Brunswick in 1800.

4.9 Opening the West

Fur traders operating out of Montreal continued to expand the frontiers in their competition with the Hudson's Bay Company. By the 1770s the traders had made it to the Saskatchewan River, and in

Boundaries of Quebec, 1763–1791

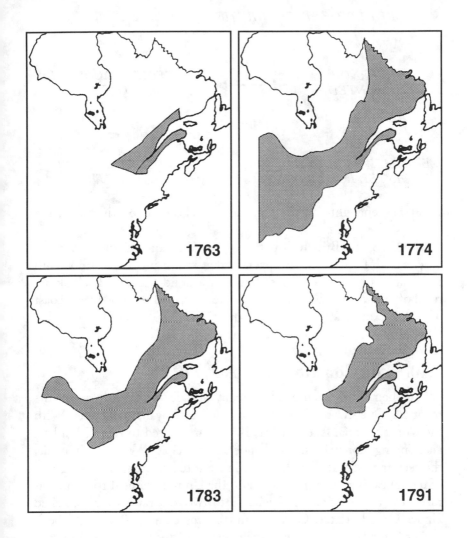

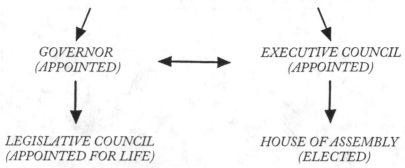

SECRETARY OF STATE FOR THE COLONIES (BRITAIN)

GOVERNOR
(APPOINTED)

EXECUTIVE COUNCIL
(APPOINTED)

LEGISLATIVE COUNCIL
(APPOINTED FOR LIFE)

HOUSE OF ASSEMBLY
(ELECTED)

1778 they encountered the continent's richest fur bearing area, the Athabaska region.

In 1776, the British dispatched Captain James Cook on yet another search for a northwest passage that might provide Europe with easier access to Asia. After sailing east around the world, Cook arrived off Vancouver Island in 1778. He described the northwest coast of North America with some accuracy and his officers left valuable accounts about the region's native peoples.

4.10 The Constitutional Act, 1791

In their third attempt in as many decades to provide a government for Quebec, the British responded to Loyalist concerns. With the Constitutional Act of 1791, Britain attempted to establish a balance among monarchical and democratic principles. William Grenville, the secretary of state for the colonies, wanted to stem the rising tide of republicanism seen in France and the United States. Provision was made for the division of Quebec into two separate colonies, called Upper Canada (later, Ontario) and Lower Canada (later, Quebec). Upper Canada was to have British common law and freehold tenure. While Lower Canada's civil law remained untouched, new areas outside the seigneurial tracts were also to be granted according to freehold tenure. The region in Quebec called the Eastern Township was the result. A seventh of all new townships in both Upper and Lower Canada were to be set aside for the benefit of a "Protestant clergy"

(clergy reserves) and another seventh as Crown land (Crown reserves).

The new government structures were weighed heavily in favour of aristocratic principles which gave emphasis to appointed positions. No laws could be passed without the consent of the governor general in Lower Canada or lieutenant-governor in Upper Canada. Governors reported to the British secretary of state for the colonies. By virtue of revenues from land sales set aside by the Constitutional Act and from other income flowing to the Crown, governors enjoyed a small measure of financial autonomy.

Governors also appointed an executive council to provide advice. Members of the upper house, called the legislative council, were appointed for life. Members of both councils often received large grants of land in an attempt to create a colonial aristocracy.

The house of assembly constituted the popular element in the structure and it had to approve all internal taxes ("money bills"). The franchise for voters was more liberal than in England, and there were no major property qualifications for people wanting to be elected. Anyone with a forty-shilling freehold in rural areas or who owned property with a yearly value of five British pounds might vote, but this disenfranchised many urban labourers and domestics. Only in 1834 did Quebec's assembly specifically disenfranchise women due to electoral violence.

A special oath of allegiance was devised to allow Roman Catholics to vote and to hold office in Lower Canada, which placed them in a better position than co-religionists elsewhere. A law passed in Prince Edward Island allowed Catholics to own land, but not vote, and New Brunswick disenfranchised Catholics until 1810. Newfoundland was not given an assembly until 1832 due to its large Roman Catholic population, but such disabilities were eventually removed throughout the British empire by 1829.

CHAPTER 5

Towards Modernization
(1792–1815)

5.1 Immigration

While the new colony in Upper Canada attracted immigrants, others moved to the Atlantic provinces, where timber exports and shipbuilding augmented the region's traditional reliance on fishing. Quebec's economy underwent profound changes during the Napoleonic Wars, and deep political divisions there and on Prince Edward Island brought to the fore the first groups resembling political parties. The coming War of 1812 was to be felt mainly in Upper Canada, where it had far-reaching effects. In the West, new rivalries between the Montreal-based North West Company and the Hudson's Bay Company resulted in violence in the Red River colony of southern Manitoba.

During the War of 1812, immigration into the British North American colonies remained modest. Nonetheless, over time immigrants added to the increasing diversity of the population and caused population levels to swell considerably. Between 1791 and 1812 Upper Canada's population grew from 14 000 to 75 000, a 500 percent rise. Atlantic Canada, meanwhile, received an influx of immigrants from the British Isles, originating primarily in Ireland and the Scottish Highlands. Newfoundland was particularly attractive to the Irish. New arrivals came increasingly in extended family units. Britain did not encourage emigration and few immigrants benefited from government assistance. Most new arrivals embarked on farming and fishing, but many pursued other forms of economic activity at the same time.

5.2 The Impact of the French Revolution on Quebec

The outbreak of the revolution in France in 1789 served to bind Quebec's elites to the British regime. In reaction to republicanism and anti-clericalism seen across the Atlantic, the clergy and seigneurs of Lower Canada transferred their allegiance to British institutions.

5.3 Early Upper Canada

Upper Canada's first lieutenant-governor, John Graves Simcoe, wanted to turn the colony into a little England with British names, a colonial aristocracy, and Anglicanism as the established church. Only in 1798 was the right to solemnize marriages extended to Lutheran, Calvinist, and Church of Scotland ministers; Methodist preachers were excluded until 1831.

Concerned with colonial defence, Simcoe moved the colony's capital to Toronto, which he renamed York, and raised an infantry corps called the Queen's Rangers. A militia bill was passed that required enlistment of men aged 16 to 50. In Upper Canada, township officials were appointed rather than elected. Large grants of land, sometimes amounting to 1200 to 2000 hectares, were given to members of the executive and legislative councils in order to foster a local aristocracy. Two military highways, Yonge and Dundas Streets, were constructed.

With Simcoe's support, the Upper Canadian legislature provided for an eventual end to slavery in 1793. No new slaves were to be brought into the province, and slave children were to be freed when they reached the age of 25. After Britain abolished the slave trade in 1807, slavery died out throughout the British colonies.

Despite Simcoe's grand design, early Upper Canadians were primarily American in origin and diverse in their religious affiliations. The Methodist, Anglican, and Presbyterian churches each commanded the allegiance of about 20 percent of the population, with a smaller number being Roman Catholics.

5.4   Resource-Based Economies and Societies

Beginning in 1791, Britain passed legislation, called the Corn Laws, that established a system of preferential duties for colonial wheat. The Corn Laws gave colonial grain a competitive advantage in the British market until free trade in 1846. Wheat exports in Lower Canada expanded significantly, and provided the main cash income for Upper Canadian farmers.

Economic growth in the Maritimes began with conflicts between France and England that erupted in war in 1793. When Britain and France imposed mutual blockades on each other in 1806, American president Thomas Jefferson closed American ports in protest. While the policy backfired in the United States, it provided greatly increased trading opportunities for the Maritimes. Although Nova Scotia's carrying trade with the British West Indies had declined in the 1790s, it expanded rapidly under these conditions. Britain encouraged the trade by paying bounties on fish exported from Nova Scotia and New Brunswick to their West Indian possessions. In Newfoundland, the transition from migratory to resident fishery was completed. By 1815, local people owned most of the fishing fleet and produced the entire salt fish yield.

When Napoleon closed the Baltics in 1807, Britain turned to its colonies to supply the timber it needed in large quantities for its navy. By 1825, New Brunswick supplied 40 percent of Britain's timber requirements. Wheat and timber far outdistanced the export of furs from Quebec by 1810. Shipbuilding was one of the most important spin-offs of the timber trade, particularly in the Maritime provinces and at Quebec. Differential duties on timber afforded the colonies a distinct price advantage until 1842.

New economic activities expanded the number of merchants and artisans throughout the colonies. Sometimes entrepreneurs made common cause with the governing elite. Licences to cut on Crown land were expensive and connections with the government were needed.

Economic expansion demanded new strategies that might produce larger business fortunes. In Lower Canada, for instance, fur trader Peter McGill diversified his interests to become a timber exporter, a shipowner, a forwarder of goods to Upper Canada, a banker, and eventually a railroad promoter. Samuel Cunard, who began work in the Halifax firm of his father, developed sawmills with impressive production on the Miramichi River in northeastern New Brunswick.

Apart from shipbuilding, manufacturing remained centred in small artisanal shops producing goods and services for local consumption. Some resources processing developed: grain was distilled into whisky, brewed into beer, and milled as flour. Trees were sawn into lumber and reduced to potash.

5.5 Fur-Trade Rivalries and the Rise of the Métis

From the 1790s, the fur trade out of Montreal was managed chiefly by the North West Company. Always searching for new areas in which to trade, Nor'Wester Alexander Mackenzie reached the Pacific Ocean in 1793. Simon Fraser descended to the coast in 1808 on the river that now bears his name and David Thompson travelled down the Columbia River three years later. After 1814, the North West Company largely controlled the Pacific fur trade that had previously been conducted by Americans.

When fur traders married Indian women, a new population of Métis developed in the Canadian West. Marriage might bring traders fresh sources of furs from their adopted families. Indian wives prepared the pemmican—the essential food for travelling—and made snowshoes and moccasins for their husbands. The women also served as interpreters for the traders. A unique Métis culture developed. From the Europeans, Indian wives learned to make a baking powder biscuit called bannock. The Métis invented the Red River cart. Made entirely of wood and leather, the efficient vehicle converted quickly to a raft for fording rivers. By the early nineteenth century, the North West Company was sheltering some 1000 women and their offspring at its posts. The Métis combined Indian and European idioms to create new languages in addition to the languages of their forebears. More Métis claimed French than English or Gaelic ancestry. After 1800, encampments of French and Métis developed at the juncture of the Red and Assiniboine rivers (present-day Winnipeg).

5.5.1   Selkirk's Red River Settlement

Having settled Scottish Highlanders on Prince Edward Island

and conducted a less successful experiment in Upper Canada, the Earl of Selkirk decided to begin a new agricultural colony for emigrants at Red River. With associates, Selkirk bought into the Hudson's Bay Company and then in 1811 secured a large land grant from corporate holdings in Rupert's Land. Selkirk's first colonists arrived in what was now called Assiniboia during the following year. Miles Macdonell was Selkirk's choice as first governor for the colony. To retain provisions, Macdonell ordered in 1814 that no pemmican (a Métis food of fur traders) be exported. He later placed a ban on buffalo running. Both prohibitions placed the Métis way of life in jeopardy.

Encouraged by the Nor'Westers to respond, the Métis succeeded in forcing Macdonell to surrender in 1815 and he was sent to Montreal. His successor, Robert Semple, was equally insensitive to them and they formed a militia under Cuthbert Grant. The Métis seized pemmican from Hudson's Bay Company posts. When surprised by Semple at Seven Oaks in 1816, an incident occurred where the governor and 20 HBC men were killed, but Grant lost only two people. Selkirk captured the North West Company's post at Fort William (Thunder Bay) in retaliation. Although he reached Red River, ill-health and his own complicity in what had transpired forced Selkirk to leave Canada.

These and other such events forged a stronger collective identity among the Métis as a "New Nation." French Canadians arrived in 1818 to establish nearby St. Boniface. Competition had become so ruinous for both fur-trading organizations that the North West Company merged into the Hudson's Bay Company in 1821. The fur trade out of Montreal came to an end.

5.6   The Beginnings of Political Parties

Only in Lower Canada and Prince Edward Island did groups resembling political parties emerge before the War of 1812. Following the implementation of the Constitutional Act in Quebec in 1792, seigneurs and merchants managed to gain a strong foothold in the House of Assembly as well as to dominate the Executive and Legislative Councils. After 1800, French Canadian professionals such as doctors, notaries, lawyers, and surveyors were elected increasingly.

Often emanating from rural agrarian backgrounds, the French Canadian professionals increasingly saw their interests—and those of the majority of Lower Canadians—as distinct from the policies of the British governors and the councils, where seigneurs and English-speaking merchants were influential. As some were strongly influenced by Enlightenment ideas and espoused a mild anticlericalism, the Roman Catholic hierarchy identified these new politicians as a challenge to its close association with the executive and its own claims to leadership.

Conflicts in Lower Canada between commercial interests, represented by English-speaking merchants, and French Canadians in the House of Assembly found expression first in 1805 when the Executive Council proposed to pay for new jails through a land tax. The majority in the House of Assembly, that came to call itself the *Parti Canadien,* suggested instead a tariff on goods entering and leaving the colony. Since one form of taxation fell more heavily on French Canadian agriculturalists and the other more fully on merchants, divisions became predicated on both social class and ethnicity. When the Assembly voted for import duties, the merchants appealed all the way to London. A newspaper called *Le Canadien,* edited by Pierre Bédard, was begun to express the views of the majority.

The situation deteriorated further after the arrival of Governor James Craig in 1807. Confusing the Canadians with the European French, Craig twice dissolved the assembly in short order and called elections in vain attempts to lessen the *Canadien* majority. In this turmoil the Assembly attempted to expel from its midst a French Canadian judge and a Jewish merchant, Ezekiel Hart, whose son Samuel later became the first Jew to hold a seat in a British legislature.

In 1810, the governor ordered the arrest of more than 20 of the editors and contributors to *Le Canadien* and threw them in jail on charges of sedition. The French Canadian Assemblymen led by Pierre Bédard began to speak of themselves as the representatives of "the Canadian nation." Political disputes had fomented the first significant signs of French Canadian nationalism. This initial round of controversy did not abate until Craig was recalled in 1811 and replaced by George Prevost, a governor who was more sensitive to balancing interest groups.

The land question dominated the early politics of Prince Edward Island, but it was the desire to elect new and independent members to the House of Assembly that led to the creation of the Loyal Electors in 1809. As groups resembling political parties were still considered as conspiratorial, the British government suppressed the Loyal Electors.

5.7   The War of 1812

The War of 1812 became the last of the colonial wars involving Canadian soil—and resulting from conflicts emanating from abroad. Relations between Britain and the United States had remained strained following the peace of 1783. To search for deserters from the royal navy, Britain employed its superior naval strength to stop American vessels. War had almost occurred in 1807 when the British opened fire on the American ship *Chesapeake* and had captured four men, three of whom were Americans. Further antagonisms arose when Tecumseh, a Shawnee Indian chief, and his brother succeeded in forming a new Indian confederacy in the West. When Tecumseh began war in 1811, many Americans suspected British complicity incorrectly, but "War Hawks" in Congress urged the United States to capture Upper Canada. The two countries went to war after Napoleon's continental system closed Europe to Britain and the British responded with a naval blockade that prevented the United States from trading with France.

5.7.1   Military Events

Tecumseh and hundreds of warriors joined the British under Major-General Isaac Brock in Upper Canada in 1812. While Brock encountered difficulties in mustering local militia and the Upper Canadian legislature proved uncooperative in placing the province on a war footing, Indians and British regulars secured the fall of Detroit.

While the Canadian side had done well during the first year of the war, the Americans captured York in 1813 and launched a second assault on the Niagara Peninsula. After the Indian victory at Beaver Dams, the Americans withdrew. American captain Oliver Perry defeated the British on Lake Erie, while the Americans also overcame a combined force of regulars and Indians at Moraviantown where Tecumseh died. To the east, the British scored a victory over an American raid at Chrysler's Farm. At Châteauguay in Lower Canada, Charles-Michel de Salaberry led the French Canadian militia in forcing a numerically superior American force to retreat.

While the Americans held southwestern Ontario for the remainder of the war, the British repulsed a final attack on the Niagara Peninsula in 1814. Later that year the British took Washington, D.C. They set it afire in return for what had been done to York the previous year.

5.7.2 Return to Peace

The Treaty of Ghent ended the war in 1814 and restored the status quo. American military incursions, nevertheless, served to reinforce the identification of many Upper and Lower Canadians with Britain. Loyalty to Britain and anti-Americanism emerged in both colonies. As a result of the war, Britain and the United States concluded the Rush-Bagot agreement in 1817 whereby a limit was placed on armed vessels on the Great Lakes. A diplomatic convention the following year denied American access to the coasts of the three Maritime colonies for drying their catch. The convention also determined the Anglo-American border in the West to be the 49th parallel.

The Roman Catholic Church in Quebec, whose official status had been uncertain since the conquest of 1760, was rewarded for its active support of the British during the war. In 1817 Bishop Joseph-Octave Plessis of Quebec was named to the Legislative Council of Lower Canada. Roman Catholicism was officially recognized in that colony and the church became bonded even more fully to the executive.

Given worries that Upper Canada's population was largely American in origin, immigration from the United States into that colony was discouraged after 1814. The imperial power also sought to improve colonial defence. From 1826 to 1832 it paid for the construction of the Rideau Canal—linking Bytown (Ottawa) to Kingston—as an alternative military route to the St. Lawrence River. Costing one million pounds, the Rideau Canal became the most costly military project paid for by the British government.

5.8   The Beginnings of Political Opposition

As the executives were accorded a prominent role in British colonial governments, governors and their advisors often ruled with minimal regard to the House of Assembly. Since the concept of a loyal political opposition had not yet taken root, dissent from the executive's was often treated harshly. Apart from Lower Canada and Prince Edward Island, opposition to the executive's power most often assumed the form of individuals holding office who disagreed with prevailing practices. Such individuals were often dismissed from office or harassed.

Robert Gourlay in Upper Canada differed in that he held no office, but after his arrival in 1817 he was critical of government policies, especially as they influenced the sale of lands that had been inherited through his wife. An agrarian radical subject to periods of mental disorder, Gourlay adopted the practice from his native Scotland of distributing questions to landholders. Complaints were raised about inadequate land policies and the obstructions to settlement posed by the clergy and Crown reserves. The responses were published in the *Upper Canada Gazette* and later as the *Statistical Account of Upper Canada* (1822). Gourlay also advocated more American immigration, accused the government of favouritism in patronage, and encouraged his supporters to convoke township meetings. Twice arrested for criminal libel and acquitted, the executive ordered him out of the province, invoking the Alien Act of 1804 that provided banishment for anyone disturbing the colony's tranquillity. When he refused, Gourlay was jailed for eight months before he departed in 1819.

CHAPTER 6

Reform and Rebellions

6.1   Colonial Oligarchies

After 1820, the political life of the British North American colonies was characterized by increasing discord. Discontent stemmed from a desire to transcend an anachronistic form of government in which the executive—and hence, the colonial oligarchies associated with it—exercised great influence. A variety of groups hoped for a fuller expression of democracy including: newly prominent merchants, landowners, professional people, and religious leaders in non-established churches. Inspired by developments in the United States and Britain, reformers advocated changes in colonial governments through a shift in power towards the elected representatives in the House of Assembly. While demands for reform varied in each colony, armed rebellions against governmental authority erupted in 1837 and 1838 in Upper and Lower Canada.

Each of the colonial capitals was dominated by relatively small numbers of office holders, military officials, and merchants. The prominence that these individuals held in colonial societies derived in varying degrees from their position in relation to political power and their wealth. As British North America lacked an aristocracy, social status rested on influence in government and wealth.

Colonial governors stood at the apex of society in both political and social realms. No laws were passed without the governor's approval as well as the assent of the (legislative) council and House of Assembly. A governor might withhold assent pending a decision from Britain. Even with these considerable powers, the governor's position was unenviable because he was expected to represent simultaneously the interests of the British Crown and the local government. A governor's only hope for quiet tenure rested in dominating both houses of the local legislature, but in recommending appointments to their upper house (or council), members of the Assembly often took offense when opponents were elevated and their own supporters were not. While popularly elected, Assemblymen were not paid for their service. The political system thereby institutionalized social tensions.

The political élites on the councils—who were often rewarded with large grants of land—were called the "Family Compact" in Upper Canada, although they did not belong to one family. They were also frequently called Tories, but referred to themselves as Constitutionalists.

Relatively few individuals had the right connections, wealth, influence, and education to be part of the colonial oligarchy. Although some were related by marriage, the tendency toward oligarchy in British North America is better viewed as a high-powered network of individuals and families able to exercise political power. In the main they feared the republicanism of France and the United States. They also vaunted the British connection and the monarchy, referring frequently to "loyalty," and stressing the need for a balance of interests in government. They supported institutions such as banks and large-scale economic projects such as canals. Generally disposed towards religion, the colonial oligarchies favoured more established churches—the Roman Catholic Church in Lower Canada and the Anglican Church there and in Upper Canada. In Lower Canada, wealthy English-speaking merchants, known collectively as the "Chateau Clique," dominated the colony's Executive Council.

In Upper Canada about half the colonial oligarchy consisted of descendants of Loyalist families. The other half had emigrated from Britain.

6.2   Moderate Reform in Upper and Lower Canada

Too sharp a distinction between the colonial oligarchies and reform advocates should not be drawn, because reformers were also part of the governing élite. Louis-Joseph Papineau, who became Speaker of the Lower Canadian Assembly in 1815—and replaced Pierre Bédard as leader of the *Canadien* party in 1819—was a lawyer and a seigneur. In Lower Canada, reform was closely associated with the rise of a new French Canadian professional élite composed of doctors, lawyers, and notaries. This group associated its own struggle with the national interests of Lower Canada and viewed itself as the people's leaders. Yet in both Lower and Upper Canada those with Irish and American backgrounds were also prominent among the reform leadership. E.B. O'Callaghan in Lower Canada and Robert Thorpe, Joseph Willcocks, and William Baldwin in the upper province came from Irish backgrounds, while Robert Nelson, Wolfred Nelson, and T.S. Brown in Quebec and Marshall Spring Bidwell in Upper Canada had lived in the United States. On the other hand, the Toronto printer William Lyon Mackenzie and John Neilson, the owner of the *Quebec Gazette,* were Scots, while Dr. John Rolph of Upper Canada had been born in England.

During the 1830s, the reform cause split into moderate and radical sections. Moderate reformers proposed greater political democracy and opposed the aristocratic nature of the constitution because they thought it contrary to the nature of Canadian society. Generally advocating an elected upper house (or legislative council), they also wanted to make appointments to the executive more representative of the political spectrum and more responsive to the House of Assembly.

A principal reform aim became the control over all government revenues—to reduce the executive's independence. Whereas Britain preferred to have colonial assemblies vote a permanent civil list, reformers advocated closer control over expenditures by voting the civil list annually. They also detected a major problem in the judiciary's lack of independence from the Crown. The chief justice sat on the executive council and other judges on the legislative council over which the chief justice presided. The land grants and other rewards received by the colonial oligarchies were also denounced. Moreover, reformers saw favouritism in the practice of using land companies as settlement promoters. They believed that such agents increased the cost of land to settlers, but in Lower Canada these grants to British companies further increased the resentment.

Although proponents of political democracy, early nineteenth century reformers should not be confused with those who advocated greater social democracy much later. Still, they tended to oppose the development of the commercial capitalism associated with banks and canal building.

In Lower Canada, the picture was clouded further by the nationalist concerns of the *Canadien* party. As the professionals at its head saw themselves as leading a distinct people, they defended the seigneurial system as a national institution when it was challenged by English-speaking business people. In this way nationalism became a vehicle by which political concerns were carried into the larger realm of society. While members of this party were Roman Catholics in the main, *Canadien* aspirations to leadership of French Canadian society led to conflict with the Catholic bishop of Quebec and the church's hierarchy over the question of elementary schools. The sources of conflict in Lower Canada were therefore more complex than anywhere else in British North America.

6.2.1 Ministerial Responsibility, Responsible Government, and the Concept of a Loyal Opposition

The various antagonisms that emerged in the politics of Lower and Upper Canada led reform leaders to advocate changes in order to make government operate more smoothly. At the heart of these proposals stood the idea of increasing the powers of the Assembly and making the governor and executive more responsive to the lower house.

While some reform advocates spoke the need for Britain and the colonial governors to act more responsibly by making appointments to the councils more representative, only a few politicians thought more deeply about how the political system might evolve. In 1807 Pierre Bédard, the leader of the *Canadien* party in Lower Canada, became the first person to expound the idea of ministerial responsibility. He thought that only by creating a ministry enjoying the confidence of the Assembly might the English-speaking control of the executive be overcome. In 1808, the Lower Canadian Assembly debated the principle of the joint responsibility of ministers. When such a ministry lost the confidence of the majority in the Assembly, Bédard wrote, the house would be dissolved, an election held, and a new ministry called in accordance with the nation's decision voiced at the polls.

While Bédard's advocacy of ministerial responsibility was innovative in the Canadian context, it was also revolutionary because it implied a diminution in the governor's role and left open the question as to how a governor might implement British policies in the face of opposition from a majority of elected members. Still, Dr. William Baldwin developed the idea further in Upper Canada in 1828: Baldwin and his son Robert came to advocate that the governor choose his executive only from among the leaders of the majority in the Assembly. William Baldwin understood responsible government as implying the existence of at least two political parties: a governing party and an opposition to keep the government in check. The idea of an effective though loyal opposition party thus began to enter political thinking, albeit slowly.

By limiting the purview of responsible government to local affairs, Baldwin helped to clarify what the governor's new role would be, but several more decades were needed to fully unravel the full implications of responsible government. Upper and Lower Canada enjoyed neither ministries nor Cabinets. Executive councils were composed of non-political officials and political advisors, who were generally not members of the House of Assembly. In the long term, to instill local self-government, agreement would have to be reached over: the separation of imperial and local affairs; and the creation of government departments headed by political advisors and administered by non-political officials as civil servants.

6.2.2 Political Disputes in Upper and Lower Canada

Controversy erupted in 1826 over the *Naturalization Bill*, which refused British citizenship to Americans who had not lived in the colony for seven years, declared allegiance to the King, and renounced their allegiance to the United States. A new act conferred citizenship automatically on those residing in the province before 1820, and provided a waiting period of seven years for others desiring to become citizens. But the controversy had created deep political divisions.

Animosities returned in 1822 when Governor Dalhousie agreed with some Lower Canadian merchants that commercial and political interests would best be served by uniting the two Canadas. Bringing the English-speaking population of the lower province together with that of the upper would help to overcome French Canadian opposition and assist the commercial development of the St. Lawrence-Great Lakes waterway. Although Louis-Joseph Papineau and the *Canadiens* thwarted this design by pleading their case in London, bitterness remained. Governor Dalhousie found his relations with the majority in the Assembly so difficult that he called a hotly contested election in 1827. Symptomatic of heightened tensions, the *Canadiens* changed their name to *Parti patriote*. When they won a majority again, as they did in every election, Britain recalled Dalhousie and replaced him with a more compliant governor, Sir James Kempt. When immigrants brought cholera in 1832, popular spokesmen demanded Britain institute tight controls on immigration, if not an outright ban. Violence reached new heights during elections in 1832.

6.3   The Atlantic Colonies

Revenues from the sale, leasing, and licensing of Crown lands in New Brunswick became the object of reformers' attention since they were spent by the colony's lieutenant-governor. In 1836, a deputation to the Colonial Office in London produced a compromise. The Assembly was accorded control over revenues from Crown lands in return for voting a permanent civil list guaranteeing the salaries of judges and civil servants. The executive was also made more responsive to the majority in the Assembly.

Joseph Howe hoped to bring Nova Scotia's political system in line with its British model, bestowing the same constitutional rights for colonists as were enjoyed overseas. Howe focused his criticism on the governor's Executive Council, the Council of Twelve, where Halifax's merchants exercised their influence. In 1835 Joseph Howe was charged with libel for printing a letter in his newspaper that charged Halifax's magistracy with essentially robbing the people. While

Howe's admirable defence led to acquittal, his case revealed the limits to free expression of opinion. He stood for election successfully in 1836. The following year the Assembly adopted 12 resolutions demanding sweeping reforms, including the election of the members of the Governor's Executive Council. Britain replied by splitting that body into legislative and executive sections.

William Cooper headed an agrarian-populist movement in favour of Prince Edward Island's tenants. Called the Escheat party, this group wanted large landowners stripped of their holdings and the land returned to those who worked it. Following an electoral victory for the Escheat movement in 1838, Cooper travelled to England to press for reforms but he met rebuff from colonial officials. Britain split the island's Council into legislative and executive sections in 1839. While two Assemblymen were taken into the Executive Council, Cooper's failure to resolve the land question and his own character discredited his leadership. Increasing thereafter, reform in Prince Edward Island came to focus on responsible government as the way to achieve escheat.

While in 1832, Newfoundland had become the first of the Atlantic colonies to receive a bicameral legislature, or an elected House of Assembly and an appointed legislative council, grave political difficulties led to paralysis. The conflicts were numerous: Roman Catholics versus Protestants, Irish versus English, fishers versus merchants, and liberals versus conservatives. To end the deadlock, Britain suspended the island's constitution in 1842 and created an amalgamated legislature with 11 elected members and 10 appointed. Newfoundland thereby became the only British North American colony to forfeit its assembly.

6.4 New Tensions in the Canadas

French Canada was overwhelmingly a rural society dependent on agriculture. After 1815 there were an increasing number of crop failures. The War of 1812 had also disrupted the grain train to Britain, the principal outlet for wheat, and the depression following from 1815 to 1820 lowered grain prices. The virgin soils of Upper Canada produced much higher yields of wheat that were sent down the St. Lawrence River for export or consumption in Lower Canada.

As the population continued to expand rapidly, French Canadians sought out more marginal agricultural lands and diversified into new crops. Yet disposable income tended to decline. And crop failures increased dramatically during the 1830s due to diseases and insects. Famine was reported in 1837.

Rural discontent was directed against immigrants and *les anglais*, the seigneurs who exacted rents, and sometimes against the clergy for tithes they received. Conflict in the political arena thereby struck a responsive cord in the countryside.

In Lower Canada, ethnic and linguistic divisions became institutionalized in the colony's political structures. Under leader Louis-Joseph Papineau, the *Patriotes* were returned with a majority at each election, but found themselves frustrated by the governor and councils. Papineau had initially admired British institutions, but during the 1830s, he began to lean more in the direction of republicanism, and what was termed Jacksonian democracy, following the election of Andrew Jackson in the United States in 1828. The Assembly wanted control over all major government revenues in order to deprive the governor and executive of independent action, including the appointment of public officials. It also wanted an elected Legislative Council.

In 1834 the Assembly of Lower Canada formulated its demands in the sweeping Ninety-Two Resolutions. This document called for an elective Legislative Council, an end to the governors' preference for English over French appointments, and greater control over revenue by the Assembly. In also advocating a boycott of British imports, the *Patriotes* understood that economics might be enlisted in the cause of the political struggle. When Papineau urged in 1834 that people also withdraw money from banks as well, he drew attention to the agrarian versus the commercial interests that separated the two sides in the politics of the lower province. As Papineau and the *Patriotes* grew more radical, a wedge divided them from more moderate reformers.

6.4.1 British Response to Discontent in Lower Canada

While Canadian problems received low priority in Britain, Lord Gosford was appointed as governor of Lower Canada in 1835 with instructions to investigate the impasse in the politics of Lower Canada.

Following Gosford's report, the British rejected an elected upper house and an executive council responsible to the Assembly.

6.4.2   Radical Reformers in Upper Canada

Reformers were unable to dominate the Assembly in Upper Canada as completely as they managed in Quebec. Although the first Reform majority was returned in 1828, its numbers were greatly reduced in the election of 1830. In 1834, reformers scored a sufficient victory to publish the *Seventh Report...on Grievances* in the following year. Although frequently inaccurate and full of impractical ideas, the report called for curbs on the lieutenant-governor's patronage and an elective legislative council. Debates over the adoption of the report revealed rifts within reform circles. Moderate reformers like Robert Baldwin and Methodist leader Egerton Ryerson continued to press for responsible government, but individuals like John Rolph and William Lyon Mackenzie wanted a greater application of the American elective principle in government.

Controversy surrounded the outspoken newspaperman William Lyon Mackenzie from the time that he founded the *Colonial Advocate* in Queenston in 1824. Mackenzie was elected to the Assembly in 1828. Meeting President Andrew Jackson in 1829, he became increasingly enamoured of American political practices, although he also met British reformers Jeremy Bentham, Richard Cobden, and John Bright when he visited England in 1832. More formidable in the verbal attack than in outlining comprehensive strategies, a comment derogatory of the Assembly printed in his newspaper in 1831 led that body to expel Mackenzie, only to see him re-elected, expelled again, and then returned once again. In 1834 he became Toronto's first mayor, although his municipal administration was notable mainly for the way in which he rewarded his supporters at the expense of his opponents.

William Lyon Mackenzie viewed himself as representing the agrarian cause in Upper Canada against a small commercial élite. Crop failures in Upper Canada from 1835 to 1837 made many farmers receptive to his criticisms of government.

The political situation in Upper Canada deteriorated when Sir Francis Bond Head was appointed lieutenant-governor in 1836. Head announced that responsibility for government resided in his office alone and that he planned only to consult his council. After calling an election in 1836, Head campaigned actively against the reformers, many of whom were defeated. Conservatives were charged with engaging in electoral bribery and fraud.

6.5 Rebellions in the Canadas

The *Patriotes* responded to the British rejection of an elected upper house by holding mass meetings of protest around the province. A renewal of the economic boycott of British goods was urged in some quarters, while others spoke of the need for armed resistance against the government. English-speaking defenders of the government formed loyalist associations such as the Doric Club that tried to disrupt *Patriote* meetings in Montreal. Young *Patriote* supporters organized the paramilitary Sons of Liberty (*Fils de la Liberté*) to promote their ideals. When the Doric Club and Sons of Liberty engaged in a street battle in Montreal in November of 1837, Lord Gosford ordered the arrest of Papineau and his main followers.

As the *Patriote* leaders fled to the countryside, the principal military confrontations were to the east and west of Montreal. At St. Denis, Wolfred Nelson and his supporters were victorious over British regulars, but the *Patriotes* were defeated in several other encounters.

The spark emitted by the violence in Lower Canada ignited the Upper Canadian "tinderbox." Mackenzie assembled a rag-tag army of some 400 north of Toronto. In the London district, a separate armed upheaval was organized. But thousands volunteered in support of the government and defeated the rebels easily. Mackenzie fled for the border.

The rebels along the border with the United States organized themselves into Hunters' Lodges (*Frères Chasseurs*) in order to gain strength. The United States proved unwilling to alienate Britain by offering them support. The Lower Canadian exiles, led by Robert Nelson, adopted a more radical program that called for an end to the seigneurial system. During an incursion across the border in February of 1838, Nelson declared the colony independent of Britain, but then he rushed back to the United States. Another invasion under the leadership of Wolfred Nelson in November fomented a more serious revolt. Although the *Patriotes* were defeated readily by British forces under Sir John Colborne, so much property was burned that Colborne became known as the "Old Firebrand."

William Lyon Mackenzie proclaimed a republic for Upper Canada from his refuge on the American side of the Niagara River. Throughout 1838 Upper Canada remained in a state of crisis as a series of border raids were launched. Many people in both Upper and Lower Canada were arrested, imprisoned, or deported, and others were hanged.

6.6   The Durham Report

Coming at a time when Queen Victoria had been enthroned in Britain, these upheavals required a more forceful British response than had been the case. As a result, in 1838 Lord Durham was dispatched as governor of Lower Canada to investigate the sources of the problems. With him were two individuals identified as colonial reformers. Durham's stay in the colony was short, and he resigned after less than six months in office. Nevertheless, he was won over to the need for responsible government.

The report on Canadian affairs that Durham published in 1839 recommended both self- and responsible government in a new union that would bind the Canadas into a single province. He hoped that the English-speaking minority in Lower Canada might make common cause with Upper Canada to overcome French Canadian opposition to economic development. The report was uncomplimentary to French Canada. Imbued with British ideas of progress, Durham viewed the French Canadians as backward. He hoped that education would assist their advance and expected that they would be assimilated. In his most famous line, Durham wrote that he had "expected to find a contest between a government and a people," but instead "found two nations warring in the bosom of a single state..." Colonial self-government in a new union was to be reconciled with imperial rule by retaining Britain's jurisdiction over the constitution, foreign relations, trade, and the disposal of public lands.

CHAPTER 7

The Union of the Canadas

7.1 The Act of Union, 1840

While a new political structure was imposed on Upper and Lower Canada by the Act of Union in 1840, the middle decades of the nineteenth century witnessed significant structural changes in the economies of British North America—resulting partially from developments abroad. The colonies shifted away from their transatlantic links with Britain toward a more continental economy, in which the United States figured more prominently. Important strides were taken in improving the St. Lawrence waterway during the 1840s and in building railways after 1850. Immigration remained high. Industrialization began to transform the economy and people's lives. Politically, the greatest challenges consisted of integrating French Canadians into the new political structures, achieving responsible government, and creating new political coalitions.

Britain followed Durham's advice in uniting Upper and Lower Canada into one legislature with two sections, known as Canada East and Canada West (respectively, Quebec and Ontario after 1867). Designed to submerge French Canada, the Union was a major injustice that has been described as a second conquest. Although the population of Canada East was much larger than its western counterpart (approximately 650 000 versus 450 000), the two sections were accorded an equal number of seats in the Legislative Assembly. English was to be the only language of the provincial parliament.

The British did not initially concede responsible government.

Political structures remained essentially the same as during the period from 1791 to 1840. The colonial governor continued to play a formative role in the political process, particularly as under the Union money bills could only be introduced into the legislature by a member of the government. This measure served the practical purpose of ending uncontrolled spending by members of the Assembly, but it also heightened the importance of the executive. A high property qualification was also imposed for those wishing to stand for election to the Assembly. Members of the Executive Council were nevertheless chosen increasingly from representatives in the Assembly.

7.2   Rise of a Reform Coalition

French Canadians were naturally offended by the Union, but some reform-minded people in Canada West believed that their only hopes resided in cooperation with like-minded individuals in Canada East. Francis Hincks took the first steps in establishing links with Louis-Hippolyte La Fontaine, a former *Patriote*. Robert Baldwin followed in developing a close association with the man who, in 1839, would become the Union's first governor, Lord Sydenham. Governor Charles Bagot appointed both Baldwin and La Fontaine to the Executive Council in 1842.

The next governor, Sir Charles Metcalfe, displayed Sydenham's attitudes. When he called an election in 1844, Baldwin's followers suffered a setback and a new ministry was formed under William Henry Draper that lasted until 1847. This government passed important school legislation, legal reforms, and provided for a permanent Civil List.

7.3   The End to Mercantilism

The competitive advantage that Britain had achieved through industrialization led some to question protective tariffs and other elements of the mercantilist system that had governed the first British empire. The Anti-Corn Law League in Britain argued that such tariffs increased the cost of living for Britain's workers. Beginning in 1842, Britain began to dismantle the tariffs. More dramatically, during the Great Irish Famine of 1846, the government of Robert Peel repealed the Corn Laws. While the movement of Britain towards free trade endangered the lucrative commerce that British North Americans had established, it also forced many people to think in terms of a continental rather than a transatlantic economy. In 1849, the last of the old mercantilist regulations, the Navigation Laws that had regulated shipping between the metropolis and its colonies, were also repealed.

7.4   The Achievement of Responsible Government

The loosening of economic regulations made the premise of limited colonial self-government more acceptable in the eyes of some British politicians. In the new British government of 1846, Durham's brother-in-law, Lord Grey, became Colonial Secretary. To retain imperial control, the British were now prepared to implement measures they had resisted before. Following elections in Nova Scotia, Britain instructed the Governor to form a responsible government in which Executive Council members would be drawn from only those commanding a majority in the Legislative Assembly.

The Canadas followed a similar, though more tumultuous, course. Following an election where Robert Baldwin and Louis-Hippolyte

STRUCTURE UNDER RESPONSIBLE GOVERNMENT

COLONIAL SECRETARY (LONDON)

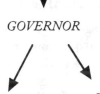

GOVERNOR

EXECUTIVE COUNCIL

LEGISLATIVE COUNCIL
(ELECTED AFTER 1856)

LEGISLATIVE ASSEMBLY

La Fontaine emerged with a majority, Governor Lord Elgin (Durham's son-in-law) called on them to form a ministry composed of their supporters—a reform coalition. While responsible government was, therefore, achieved in both colonies, it did not go unchallenged. The Rebellion Losses Bill of 1849 put the concept to the test. The legislation was intended to indemnify those who had lost property in the Lower Canadian upheavals of 1837-38, but many found it repugnant. In fact, in protest, a mob burned the House of Assembly in Montreal. Once the principle of a responsible Executive Council had been instilled, nevertheless, that body evolved into what became known as the Cabinet.

Some of the young intellectuals who had formed the *Institut Canadien* in 1844, a literary and debating society in Montreal, opposed the Union. Among its members stood earlier adherents to the discredited *Patriote* party. The newspaper associated with this position, *L'Avenir*, spoke positively of Canada becoming annexed to the United States because of American egalitarian principles. The business people felt that Britain had turned its back on Canada. The British American League felt a union of all the British North American colonies appeared as the best way of escaping what they saw as domination by the French Canadians.

7.5   New Political Parties

Controversies emerging during the 1840s and the new responsible government helped foster new political parties after mid-century. Debates over whether schools and universities were to be state run or managed by church institutions led George Brown of the Toronto *Globe* to create a Voluntaryist movement. Conceiving of the state as a totally secular institution and churches as voluntary institutions, Brown advocated that there be no sectarian schools. His followers became known as *Voluntaryists*. After the 1851 census showed that the population of Canada West had surpassed that of the East, Brown demanded representation by population ("rep by pop"). Voluntaryists tended to fear domination by Canada East.

Another reform group based in southwestern Ontario advocated populist, democratic reforms. Called *Clear Grits*, they wanted more streamlined government and a constitution based on the American

Political Parties in the Canadas Before Confederation

Canada West	Canada East
<u>Conservatives</u>	
Liberal-Conservatives	Bleus
(John A. Macdonald)	(George-Etienne Cartier)
<u>Reformers</u>	
(Forerunners of the Liberals)	
Clear Grits	Rouges
(George Brown)	(Antoine-Aimé Dorion)

model, allowing universal manhood suffrage, the secret ballot (not achieved until 1874), and more frequent elections. And Brown himself led his followers into a new Reform coalition in 1857. These Reformers shed their own advocacy of American democracy in favour of British parliamentary Liberalism. Although still often called Clear Grits, the Reform platform included "rep-by-pop," national elections, and free trade.

Similarly, a group of radical reformers called the *Rouges* appeared in Canada East in the election of 1848. The Rouges shared many areas of common concern with the Clear Grits of Canada West: the need to democratize government; the separation of church from state; and hostility to megaprojects such as the Grand Trunk Railway. Antoine-Aimé Dorion emerged as their leader, but a young Wilfrid Laurier was associated early on with the Rouges.

Yet for two decades, many differences prevented consolidation between Reformers in Canada East and West. Clear Grits were strong temperance advocates, a cause that attracted fewer adherents in Canada East. The Rouges enjoyed links with the *Institut Canadien* and drew on European rather than British liberal traditions. They viewed annexation to the United States in a positive light. These differences between the parties made the Union all the more difficult to govern. As well, many members of the Assembly continued to be independent.

Some groups coalesced. However, during the ministry of Allan McNab (a Tory) and Augustin-Norbert Morin (an old Reformer) from 1854 to 1857, the Liberal-Conservative party emerged. (Today it is called the Progressive Conservative party.) Liberal-Conservatives were closely associated with big business, advocated economic development through projects such as railways, supported close relations between church and state (including in education), and believed strongly in the maintenance of the British connection. John A. Macdonald assumed the leadership of the Liberal-Conservatives in 1856, but he always worked in close association with George-Etienne Cartier from Montreal, whose followers were known as the *Bleus*. Both Macdonald and Cartier dabbled in business themselves. Cartier, in particular, was not only the solicitor for the Grand Trunk Railway, but also the director of many banking, insurance, and mining companies.

7.6   Reciprocity and Tariffs

British North America signed a reciprocity treaty with the United States in 1854. Negotiated by Canadian governor general Lord Elgin, the agreement provided for the exchange of natural (not manufactured) products between the British North American colonies and the southern republic. The United States only agreed to the treaty in exchange for access to Atlantic Canada's fisheries. While trade with the United States increased during the 10 years that the Reciprocity Treaty lasted, central Canada benefited more fully than the Maritimes.

At the same time, however, the Union of the Canadas increased duties on specified commodities in 1843 and 1858-59. Such levies constituted an important source of government revenue.

7.7   Transportation Improvements

An expanding economy and population necessitated improvements in transportation. The Erie Canal, constructed by the Americans to connect Buffalo to New York City via the Mohawk-Hudson river system, threatened to siphon off the trade of Upper Canada after it opened in 1825. Lower Canada completed a canal around the Lachine rapids near Montreal in 1825, but the Welland Canal to circumvent Niagara Falls was a much larger undertaking. It was subsidized by both the Upper Canada and the British governments, and was opened in 1829.

The government of the Union undertook to improve the St. Lawrence River system. The Welland and Lachine canals were improved, while rapids and shallow waters were overcome through various other canals. These works, completed in 1848, renewed rivalry between the ports of Montreal and New York for control of western commerce. The United States passed Drawback Acts in 1845-46 to allow Canadian imports and exports to pass through American territory duty free.

Steam transportation also became increasingly important, but development stretched over many decades. In 1809 John Molson Sr. had launched the first steamship built in Lower Canada. In 1840, Samuel Cunard of Halifax succeeded in gaining the main contract for a steamship service between Britain and North America. By mid-century, iron-hulled vessels and steamships were able to navigate the St. Lawrence as far as Montreal. As steam power slowly became more important than sail in oceanic commerce, the Maritimes would, as a result, eventually experience economic difficulties.

Railways were to prove even more important. Even though the first short railway had been constructed in Lower Canada in 1836, developments in this area were rapid only after 1850. Two legislative acts paved the way for fast, albeit costly, expansion. The first was the Guarantee Act of 1849, allowing the Union government to guarantee the interest on half the bonds financing the construction of rail-lines of more than 120 kilometres in length. Second, a municipal act allowed municipalities to lend railway companies money to build within their jurisdictions. Once the Union also began a Municipal Loan Fund in 1852, towns and villages vied with each other to attract the dual ribbons of steel. Telegraphs started to follow the new railway lines. After the first telegraph service linking Canada with the American system was completed in 1847, developments in this area were also rapid.

Four railways were especially important. The St. Lawrence and Atlantic provided Montreal with an ice-free port in Portland, Maine, after 1853. When finished two years later, the Great Western Railway travelled from Niagara Falls via London to Windsor. Able to capture part of the trade of the American midwest, the Great Western proved profitable. Its president, Sir Allan McNab, coined the memorable phrase characterizing contemporary political culture: "All my politics are railroads." The Northern Railway went through some of Ontario's most important agricultural land from Toronto to Collingwood.

Central Canadians became fervent railway builders, and their foremost line, the Grand Trunk, emerged as the longest in the world. Formed in 1852—with its main track completed by 1859—the Grand Trunk ran from Sarnia to Quebec City. The railway's finances raised a furor. Most of the capital was British, but the railway was also heavily dependent on influential politicians in government. When plans to develop a link with Halifax fell through, the Grand Trunk purchased the St. Lawrence and Atlantic Railway. Although construction of the Victoria Bridge across the St. Lawrence was considered an engineering marvel when it opened officially in 1860, Montreal remained unable to upstage New York City. Meanwhile, the Canadian government assumed a large public debt to support railway construction, much of it in support of the Grand Trunk. Between 1852 and 1867 over 3200 kilometres of track were laid, and over $100 million was spent on railways.

7.8   Industrialization

Before 1850, most manufacturing was dispersed geographically, and took place in small shops supplying local markets. Cities functioned primarily as commercial centres for their immediate hinterlands or concerned themselves with the import/export trade. Most industries had engaged in making textiles, blacksmithing, and serving the resource trades. Only shipbuilding was a large-scale industry, with seven shipyards in Quebec City employing over 1300 people by mid-century.

During the 1850s the Canadas experienced a first round of industrialization linked inextricably with railway development. By the 1860s the Canadian railway companies employed some 6600 people. Railways allowed goods and services to be distributed over a much vaster area. The rail companies themselves became major manufacturers when they began to build foundries and mills to make rails and then to construct locomotives in their own shops. Railways and industrialization thus emerged together.

Industrialization proceeded slowly and unevenly. Within Canada East, Montreal emerged as the foremost industrial centre in British North America. That city's natural geographical advantage, its numerous railway connections, and the dynamism of its entrepreneurs accounted for its lead. While few other industrial centres emerged in that colony, the pattern was different in Canada West where Toronto and several other communities experienced considerable industrial growth. The number of towns with populations between 1000 and 5000 more than doubled between 1851 and 1871. Hamilton, in particular, profited from its established links with its agricultural hinterland and from its location at the head of Lake Ontario and in relation to the new railways.

The process of industrialization proceeded slowly and unevenly. Much early industry remained rurally based, although industries tended to become concentrated in urban centres over several decades. And without there being any income tax, the productive capacities of industry created larger numbers of business people with immense wealth. By mid-century, for instance, the most affluent 10 percent of Hamilton's population held 88 percent of its wealth, while the lowest 40 percent controlled only six percent of the city's wealth. Most of the poor were undoubtedly recent immigrants, many of them Irish and Catholic.

7.8.1   The Rise of Organized Labour

Trade unions were older than industrialization but they were also greatly affected by it. Craft organizations developed early among skilled trades such as carpentry in Halifax in 1798—albeit they were isolated units concerned only with local issues. The building of canals and railways created larger work forces capable of taking collective action. Labour riots were common. Unrest was so prevalent on canal construction in the 1840s and during railway building that special police forces were created.

Business succeeded in having governments pass legislation to protect their interests. Unions were considered illegal combinations restraining trade, and various colonies passed master and servant acts that allowed courts to impose penalties (including jail terms) for workers who left their jobs.

Industrialization entailed larger concentrations of capital, factories, mechanization, and the division of work into series of specific tasks. The process of mechanization divorced workers from control of production. A shoemaker might formerly have made an entire boot, but shoe factories divided the process into a series of repetitive activities. Productivity increased greatly, while mechanization threatened traditional crafts and pride in production fell. In 1849, for instance, shoemakers in Montreal attacked a factory and destroyed sewing machines (an example of what in Britain was called Ludditism). In any event, British and American international unions appeared in the 1850s and unions with several local chapters also developed. Both allowed for more concerted collective action.

Women and girls had always contributed to agricultural production, but now they became an increasing proportion of the industrial work force. By 1871, they comprised over a third of Montreal's industrial workers and 80 percent of workers in the clothing industry. They worked for drastically lower wages than males, but were difficult to organize as so many were young women or engaged in piecework production at home. The latter became known as the "sweating system."

7.9   Boundary Adjustments

In the decades following the War of 1812, Britain grew increasingly aware of the military difficulties inherent to defending her position in North America. After the government of the United States refrained from assisting Upper and Lower Canadian rebels exiled on American soil, Britain moved towards establishing an entente with the United States.

But the vast Oregon territory on the remote Pacific coast remained contentious. In 1818, the two countries had agreed to joint occupancy of the area. After the North West Company and the Hudson's Bay Company had merged in 1821, the revitalized business enterprise sent Sir George Simpson to tap the rich natural resources of the region. Simpson established Fort Vancouver 150 kilometres north of the Columbia River. Through the creation of a number of other fur-trading depots, the Hudson Bay's Company established a British presence. Even so, increasing numbers of Americans began to enter the region in the 1830s and 1840s.

James Polk made the boundary issue in the Oregon territory one of the cornerstones for his successful bid for the American presidency during the election of 1844. Nonetheless, an Anglo-American treaty was reached in 1848, extending the 49th parallel from the Rocky Mountains to the Pacific. What would become Washington State fell below the 49th parallel, and the British government moved to make the Hudson's Bay Company its colonizing agent on Vancouver Island. A royal grant in 1849 attempted to safeguard the rights of Indians, while requiring that the company make land available to settlers at reasonable prices. With virtually free land available to the south, the white population on Vancouver Island paled in comparison. Indians remained the principal residents.

7.10 British Columbia

In 1851, James Douglas became the second governor of Vancouver Island. A man of African-Scots descent who married a Métis woman, Douglas wanted to avoid the frequent wars of the past between whites and Indians. During the 1850s, he negotiated 14 treaties with various indigenous groups on the island. The lands received by the aboriginal populations were not large, but aboriginal title was acknowledged.

The land question quickly became controversial. Indians realized that their territories were becoming more valuable than the compensation they received for them. They looked to Britain to assist them, but were refused. The government of Vancouver Island (and later, British Columbia) set aside reserves without extinguishing aboriginal title. At the same time, the indigenous population experienced rapid decline in its numbers due to European diseases. Perhaps as many as a third of Vancouver Island's Indians died within two years following the outbreak of smallpox in 1862.

James Douglas was appointed as the first governor of the mainland colony, established in 1858. It was named British Columbia by Queen Victoria. The beginning of the Fraser River gold rush, beginning in the same year, transformed the region. Douglas tried to ensure order by drawing up mining regulations, licensing miners, and hiring constables. To further exploit the interior's resources, the governor had the Cariboo Road constructed by 1863. For his efforts, James Douglas became known as the "Father of British Columbia."

Christian missionaries also became active during the late 1850s. The missionaries attempted to suppress native traditions in favour of European practices. Many Indians, in any event, adjusted to changing circumstances. Some began mixed farming, while others entered logging, served as seamen, and worked in the fishing and canning industries.

CHAPTER 8

Colonial Societies in the Early Nineteenth Century

8.1   The "Peopling" of British North America

The massive waves of immigrants arriving in British North America following the War of 1812 transformed the colonies. Towns and cities grew. Agriculture, fishing, and forest work occupied most people in the central and eastern colonies, but the development of the economic infrastructure with canal building and railway construction began to alter the lives of many. As greater emphasis came to be placed on education, the question of state versus religious responsibility arose, and religious questions became increasingly divisive in public life. The aboriginal peoples in eastern Canada were increasingly marginalized. On the Prairies, the Métis grew in numbers, but the Plains Indians experienced the ravages of European diseases. Hardships also ensued when areas were depleted of fur-bearing animals and over-hunting reduced the number of bison (buffalo) that had provided essential food and clothing.

All the British North American colonies experienced great population increases after 1815 and up to mid-century. While the population of European origin probably stood at 250 000 in 1791, it had increased to some 1.6 million people in 1845. Throughout the colonies, more Irish arrived than any other ethnic group. French Canadians—who had previously outnumbered English speakers—became a minority in the Canadas by 1851. While there had been some 50 000

Indians in the settled areas of the eastern colonies in 1791, by mid-century there were approximately 150 000 in the greater territorial reaches obtained through westward and northern movement.

The availability of cheap land and the lure of economic opportunities were the chief attractions pulling people to the colonies, although some came for religious reasons. As immigration came primarily from Britain, historians have also examined conditions in the British Isles that tended "to push" people abroad. While Britain's population had begun to expand in the late eighteenth century, landlords increased rents and converted common lands to pasture. Industrialization and the beginning of the factory system displaced traditional crafts such as weaving, making it difficult to earn a living. Ireland and parts of Scotland experienced periodic famines, and severely so in the case of Ireland in the 1840s. As the timber ships coming to the British colonies preferred paying human cargo as ballast for their return voyages to North America, a larger proportion of poor people arrived after 1815, but many immigrants represented the wealthier or more resolute sections of their home societies. Family migration became increasingly important. Most people farmed, many also practised their crafts at the same time.

There were five means of emigration and settlement:

1. *Government assistance* was only provided in limited instances to help such groups as demobilized soldiers or to reduce the excess Irish population. Some 700 Scottish emigrants received support to settle Lanark County of Upper Canada in 1816. Peter Robinson headed a government-supported assistance program that brought some Irish to the Bathurst area of New Brunswick in 1823 and around Peterborough in Upper Canada two years later. As the costs of such initiatives proved high, the British government left immigration to the private sector.

2. *Private landowners and land companies* also promoted emigration and settlement. Thomas Talbot, the best know of these private proprietors, came to own or control hundreds of thousands of acres in Upper Canada after 1803. While he sold lots to new arrivals, Talbot also had to bear the costs of building roads in order to allow access to his properties.

3. *Transatlantic transportation contractors* would temporarily convert their sailing vessels to accommodate immigrant passengers for their return trip to North America.
4. *Voluntary associations* such as anti-slavery societies in Upper Canada and the United States helped specific groups to emigrate, although the majority of ex-slaves arrived without formal assistance. The Fugitive Slave Act of 1850 in the United States increased this movement in favour of Upper Canada because it allowed slave owners to pursue escaped slaves into non-slave states, thus forcing larger numbers across the international border.
5. *Unassisted immigrants* were more common than any other, but conditions on the ocean crossing were frequently terrible, especially after 1825 when the British government stopped trying to regulate the passage in any significant way. In the 1830s and 1840s, one in 28 immigrants died on board ship.

Immigration reached new heights during the 1840s and 1850s. Many of the arrivals came from Ireland, a country that had been suffering the effects of overpopulation and periodic famine for many years due to its excessive reliance on one crop, potatoes. The Great Famine of 1846 sent unprecedented numbers of Irish to British North America in the following year.

While some immigrants moved on to the United States and others initially crowded into cities—particularly in Canada East—many of the Irish succeeded over the longer term in becoming farmers in the rural areas of Canada West. Economic depression temporarily reduced the number of immigrants in 1848, but a large flow resumed once prosperity returned in succeeding years. In contrast to the United States, pre-Confederation Irish emigration to the Canadas was characterized by having a higher proportion drawn from the island's northern counties and a higher percentage who were Protestants. The population of the Canadas grew from 1.1 million in 1841 to almost 2.0 million in 1851.

With its proximity to the American border and its agricultural lands not yet fully occupied, Canada West emerged as the end point of a network that assisted slaves flee to freedom. Josiah Henson, an ex-slave who had escaped to Upper Canada in 1830, became the leading spirit behind the best known colony of African-Americans near Chatham. Henson was reputed to have been the inspiration for the key figure in Harriet Beecher Stowe's anti-slavery novel, *Uncle Tom's Cabin*. In 1851, the same year in which the novel was published, Canadian abolitionists created the Canadian Anti-Slavery Society to assist refugees. While up to 40 000 of Canada West's residents may have claimed African ancestry by 1860, they encountered severe discrimination at the hands of white society. School legislation in 1850 permitted racially segregated schools, but only when those of African descent requested. After Abraham Lincoln's Emancipation Proclamation in 1863, many returned to the United States. In 1862, the *Homestead Act* in the United States provided free grants in the midwest that siphoned off immigrants south of the border following the conclusion of the Civil War in 1865.

8.1.1 Epidemics

Immigrants sometimes brought epidemics to the colonies. After cholera flared in Quebec in 1832, a quarantine station was established down river from Quebec City. Other major cholera epidemics erupted in 1834, 1849, and 1854.

Among no other peoples were the effects of epidemics more savage than aboriginal peoples. Smallpox raged among the Indians of the Canadian Plains several times. An epidemic of this disease in 1837-38 reduced the Assiniboine people by two-thirds, from nine to three thousand. Such devastations altered population balances and led the Crees to emerge as the largest people in the region. Scarlett fever, measles, and whooping cough reaped additional havoc. Seeing the aboriginal peoples fleeing northward, the Hudson's Bay Company began the first extensive vaccination program among the western Canadian Indians.

8.1.2 Effects of Rising Populations

Before Confederation, the British North American colonies remained overwhelmingly rural. Most people earned their living through farming, fishing, and lumbering. At mid-century, many married women might still expect to bear six or seven children in their lifetimes.

The effects of rising population were experienced everywhere. Irish immigrants constituted a large part of the labour force that constructed the new canals. French Canadian emigration to the New England states reached new highs in the 1840s and 1850s. Geographical mobility ("transiency") was also high within Canada. Eastern Townships and Lac Saint-Jean regions of Canada East opened up. Although historians have so far been able to ascertain that those who remained permanently in rural areas were able to prosper in the main, the fate of those moving remains to be explored fully. Towns and cities also grew significantly.

Religious animosities involving Roman Catholics and Protestants flared. Economic rivalries between Irish and French Canadians competing for jobs in the Ottawa valley timber industry in the late 1820s and 1830 erupted in the Shiners' Wars. During the period of the Union government after 1840, religious controversy in the political arena centred around sectarian control of public schools and other institutions such as orphanages, asylums, and hospitals.

8.1.3 Native Peoples

In the Atlantic provinces, Micmacs were given provisions and unsurveyed local reserves, but their lands were subject to severe squatting by the white population. European diseases continued to exact such a high price in human lives that the last member of the Beothuk people of Newfoundland died in 1820.

In Upper Canada, the British government continued the tradition of land settlements with the country's native peoples. After 1818, the provincial government changed the method of purchasing land: annual payments, or annuities in perpetuity, were introduced as an alternative to the lump sum offer. As white society expanded, Indians in Upper and Lower Canada moved northward or became increasingly marginalized. Several thousand Anishinaberg—Ojibwas, Odawa (Ottawa), and Powawatomi—also moved into Upper Canada in the 1830s and 1840s. Lieutenant-Governor Francis Bond Head negotiated their removal to Manitoulin Island in Lake Huron in 1836 and 1837. Most of the Oneidas (one of the Six Nations), who had remained in American territory, purchased land on the Thames River near London after 1840.

Indians soon resented the foreign intrusion and corruption rampant in Indian administration. Many converted to Christianity when denominations such as Methodism employed native preachers. Reserves were surveyed and schools provided. After 1830, government programs aimed at "civilization" (assimilation) and Christianization, the former a response to what was perceived as a dying way of life. After the conduct of native affairs was transferred from British to colonial responsibility, the Union government passed "An Act for the Gradual Civilization of the Indian Tribes in the Canadas" in 1857. Aboriginal peoples found much that was objectionable in this legislation. Without consultation, it defined who was to be considered Indian, and the criteria outlined for the enfranchisement of native peoples were so high that almost no Indians became citizens.

Some Indians such as the Blackfoot people of present-day Saskatchewan saw their existence transformed through the horses, iron, and firearms that filtered first from Europeans to aboriginal neighbours. They traded pemmican with the Hudson's Bay Company and heavy buffalo hides with the American Fur Company to the south. When the latter business collapsed suddenly in 1864, many independent whisky traders invaded. Social disorder resulted.

8.1.4 The Western Métis

In the early nineteenth century, the Métis population began to double every 15–20 years. While divided by particular ancestries, the mixed-bloods developed a distinctive identity. When they went on their buffalo hunts twice annually, they elected a general council. While one of this number became chief or governor, captains were also appointed to supervise the hunt.

Other developments contributed to the formation of collective consciousness. Holding an effective monopoly of the western trade, the Hudson's Bay Company lowered its prices for furs and pemmican. When the Métis turned to trading with the Americans, thus offending what the Hudson's Bay Company claimed to be its exclusive trade rights, Pierre-Guillaume Sayer was charged in 1849 with illicit trafficking. When Sayer was convicted but no sentence was rendered, the Métis enjoyed a great victory for the freedom of trade. Two years later, at the battle of Grand Coteau in Montana, the Métis also defended themselves successfully against their Sioux adversaries by drawing their carts, packs, and saddles into a circle.

Métis life changed in a variety of ways. The Red River area's isolation ended as Métis travelled in larger numbers to trade at St.

Paul in Minnesota. Mail service arrived in 1853 and a railway reached St. Paul in 1853. Beginning in 1859 steamboats began to run regularly between the American town and Red River. As the buffalo declined due to over hunting, beginning in the 1860s some Métis moved further west to present-day Saskatchewan and Alberta.

8.2   Economic Development

An aspect of economic development was the growth of banking. The creation of the Bank of Montreal in 1817, the Bank of New Brunswick in 1820, the Bank of Upper Canada in 1821, and the Halifax Banking Company in 1825 symbolized the great economic expansion that had occurred. As banks were as yet solely commercial ventures—not intended for the general public—they were viewed suspiciously by reformers who saw them as bastions of privilege. With industrialization, banks continued to flourish.

8.2.1   Land Policies and Settlement

Just as the British government had granted land to the Loyalists and to disbanded soldiers, it was a common practice for colonial governors to reward officials, contractors, and military officers with large tracts of land. As individual settlers could not gain easy access to virgin forest, the government in Lower Canada after 1791 initially favoured the "leader and associate" system. In return for settling associates on new lands, leaders received additional grants to offset their costs. In reality, many of the leaders, who were wealthy merchants, provided the government with inflated lists of settlers and provided few services.

The decision to sell large tracts to land companies also created controversy. As well, the provisions in the Constitutional Act requiring that one-seventh of newly opened lands be set aside as Crown reserves and another seventh as reserves in support of a "Protestant clergy" created additional friction. While the Anglican Church in Upper Canada contended that clergy reserves were intended for their support as the established church in England, other religious groups disagreed, particularly Presbyterians who constituted the established church in Scotland, and Lower Canadian Roman Catholics who had grown accustomed to close relations between their denomination and the state.

8.2.2 Urban Growth

While most people settled on the land, towns and cities also grew. Quebec City's population expanded at a rate of five percent a year in the first half of the nineteenth century. Trade promoted urban growth, but cities such as Saint John and Montreal were home to a variety of industries based on production in small shops. Most towns per se spread over only limited areas close to their waterfronts. The foremost cities were also centres of political activity where soldiers were garrisoned.

With 22 500 people in 1825 and 40 000 in 1840, Montreal emerged as British North America's most important city. Its commerce was dominated by English-speaking merchants who created a committee of trade in 1821 that evolved into a board of trade by 1842. Economic activity diversified away from fur trading to grain exporting, timber trading, and manufacturing. John Molson was one of the city's pioneer industrialists. He imported barley seed from England and distributed it to farmers to provide grain for his brewery. Molson was elected to the Assembly of Lower Canada, sat on the Legislative Council, and was president of the Bank of Montreal. He revealed the variety of interests characteristic of business in this period. Workers produced leather goods, barrels, clothing, and beer. Women and immigrants worked principally as domestic servants in Montreal and elsewhere, although some eked out an existence by making dresses and hats for the wealthy.

English-speaking merchants, intent on keeping property taxes low, dominated civic administrations in Montreal and Quebec City. Various workers organized for mutual protection, but they seldom went on strike.

Urban conglomerations prompted sanitary and other innovations. Saint John constructed a wooden sewer system, but few people connected to it before 1840 because a fee was charged. The addition of a piped water supply during the same decade reduced the risks resulting from serious fires. Aqueducts were first introduced in Montreal in 1801 to supply drinking water; in 1819 they were converted to cast-iron pipe. Oil lamps were introduced into that city in 1815 and gas lighting after 1830. Most other colonial towns lacked such amenities. Policing remained rudimentary. A few ward constables and the night watch generally sufficed for security.

8.3 Religion

A wide variety of religious groupings was one of the most notable features of colonial life.

Roman Catholicism was never established as fully as was the Anglican Church in England and the Presbyterian Church in Scotland. But its bishops developed close bonds with British governors after the Conquest. Bishop Joseph-Octave Plessis cemented this alliance by support for Britain during the Napoleonic Wars and the War of 1812. In 1817, he was rewarded with a seat on the Lower Canadian Legislative Council. Two years later Rome made Plessis archbishop of Quebec and created new dioceses.

For many years, the Roman Catholic hierarchy feared that the British would recognize Bishop Jacob Mountain, the first Anglican bishop to arrive in 1793, as head of an established church. Until the 1830s, the Roman Catholic hierarchy tolerated the governor's involvement in the appointment of its bishops and parish priests. But slowly, the church felt secure to control its own internal administration.

Bishop Plessis and other clerics viewed the rising French Canadian professional élites suspiciously, and generally sided with the executive in government. They took exception to the interest of these liberals in Enlightenment thinkers like Voltaire and Montesquieu, because they feared the anti-clericalism rampant during the French revolution. The church's human resources were not great as the number of priests declined from 200 in 1760 to 150 by 1791, although it increased to some 300 by the time of the rebellions. Plessis therefore encouraged the formation of church-related classical colleges. The first bishop of Montreal, Jean-Jacques Lartigue, went further than Plessis had by publicly denouncing those challenging governmental authority during the rebellion of 1837.

The fortunes of the Roman Catholic Church began to improve after the Union of 1840. Bishop Ignace Bourget of Montreal was able to work more cooperatively with the elected politicians of Canada East like Louis-Hippolyte La Fontaine to secure favourable legislation in the area of education. Bourget greatly augmented the clerical resources in his diocese by inviting a number of European religious orders to establish there. He tried to direct his church towards the

Papacy and introduced the Roman liturgy in services.

Following past clerical traditions, Ignace Bourget emerged as the foremost foe of the liberal thinkers who gathered in the *Institut Canadien*. Other leaders of established churches like Anglican Bishop John Strachan and Roman Catholic Bishop Alexander Macdonell of Upper Canada were equally conservative in their social views. To such, inequality seemed the natural state of human existence. While they also believed that established churches fostered the best social order, none was elevated officially to that position in any of the British North American colonies.

While the established Anglican and Roman Catholic churches valued order and hierarchy, many dissenting Protestants stressed the direct experience of God. And they objected to the preference shown the established churches by government in matters such as the solemnization of marriage. They also tended to support strong temperance measures against the consumption of alcohol and advocated strict Sabbath observance. The dissenters were diverse. Methodists, Presbyterians, Baptists, Congregationalists, Christian Universalists, Mormons, Mennonites, and Quakers differed considerably from each other. Some, such as the Methodists and Baptists, insisted on fewer educational qualifications for their ministry than the clergy in the established churches had to attain. Americans predominated among the Methodists until those in Upper Canada broke away from their parent church by creating their own Canada Conference in 1828. Many dissenters were also evangelicals who emphasized the importance of a personal conversion to Christ. Methodists in particular held camp meetings and revivals where people were encouraged to affirm their faith publicly.

8.4   Education

Establishing the rudiments of public education in British North America was complicated by the competition between religious and state authorities. The role of religion in education raised the question of which churches should play a role. Also, in Lower Canada, the situation was complicated by the fact that most Roman Catholics were French while most Protestants were English. In addition to these ethnic and church/state rivalries, other contentious issues involved the roles of local versus central authorities, and the question of financial support for schools.

While each colony worked out its own solutions to these problems, three patterns emerged: state systems such as those in New Brunswick, Nova Scotia, and Prince Edward Island; a state system with separate Roman Catholic schools funded by law, such as emerged in Canada West; and denominational systems that emerged in Canada East and Newfoundland where the Roman Catholic and Anglican churches were strong. Nova Scotia and Canada West both allowed for segregated schools for children of African descent, but they later were established within the state system only after parents of colour petitioned for such a school to begin.

In Lower Canada/Canada East, the interplay between religious and state authorities regarding education was the most intricate. The Roman Catholic Church viewed suspiciously the government's first attempt to provide public support for common (elementary) schools because it saw the influence of Anglican Bishop Jacob Mountain in the legislation. So few elementary schools were created that the church succeeded in getting the Assembly to authorize church-sponsored schools financed and directed at the parish level, and schools run by local elected officials. Disputes with clergy were frequent. In the face of church pressure, the Assembly abrogated the legislation in 1836.

During the Union from 1841 to 1867, the Roman Catholic Church was able to secure more favourable legislation, especially the School Act of 1846 providing for two state-aided denominational systems (Roman Catholic and Protestant). The province was left primarily to provide financing. The teaching profession gradually became dominated by priests, brothers, and nuns. The church also ran most of the secondary schools. The Roman Catholic Church thus emerged as a formidable force in French Canadian education.

In Upper Canada, state support for elementary education began with the Common School Act of 1846 entrusting school building to local boards. John Strachan wanted the Anglican Church recognized as the colony's established church which would have given it responsibility for education, but he met a stronger foe in the Methodist minister, Egerton Ryerson, who served as superintendent of education in Canada West from 1844 to 1876. An advocate of free, nonsectarian public education, Ryerson constructed the basis of the province's educational system during the Union of the Canadas. His Common School Act of 1846 was notable for resisting political control of education by creating a board of education, a normal school, and elected school boards for operating the schools. While Ryerson created centralized provincial control, especially in the areas of curriculum, texts, and teacher qualifications, he also provided special schools for Indians, those of African descent, and bilingual schools for such minority languages as German and French.

As the numbers of Roman Catholics in the province grew, pressures mounted for their own educational institutions apart from the Protestant ones pervading the public system. The Catholic separate system was created in a series of legislative acts between 1853 and 1864. In return for a share of provincial and municipal educational grants, the Catholic schools submitted to provincial inspection, centralized control of texts and curriculum, and provincial standards for teacher training. Ontario thus developed a state and a denominational system, but compulsory education did not arrive until 1871.

Debates over education stood among the most rancorous of the mid-century confessional controversies. No area escaped them, although some more informal educational institutions managed to stand largely apart. The controversy that erupted in Prince Edward Island over Bible reading in the schools in 1856 strongly influenced the colony's political life. The evangelical Protestants who favoured the presence of the Bible in the classroom found themselves supported by old Tories and opposed by other Protestants and Catholic Liberals. In contrast, the Mechanics Institutes that had been founded in Scotland in 1823 spread to the colonies. They took root principally in cities and towns where they provided lectures and libraries for upwardly mobile artisans and professionals. In some instances their collections provided the basis for the public libraries that emerged later in the century.

In the realm of higher education, there was no greater resolution of the conflict between church and state than among elementary schools. Religious influence was more pronounced at the advanced level. Seven universities were begun through church activities in the Maritimes between 1838 and 1855: Prince of Wales and St. Dunstan's in Prince Edward Island; Acadia, St. Mary's, Mount Saint Vincent, and St. Francis Xavier in Nova Scotia; and Mount Allison in New

Brunswick. While Dalhousie College in Halifax was established in 1818 by Governor Lord Dalhousie as a non-denominational institution, it quickly became exclusively Presbyterian in orientation.

In Upper Canada, John Strachan secured a charter for King's College, which was to be the provincial university under Church of England control. The Presbyterians established Queen's University and the Methodists ran Victoria College. In 1849 the state brought King's under government control, creating the University of Toronto the next year. In contrast to Nova Scotia where Joseph Howe called for one provincial university, various church universities in Canada West affiliated some of their denominational institutions with the secular University of Toronto. Anglicans followed this practice by creating Trinity College to replace the now defunct King's.

In Canada East, Anglophones and Protestants were better served with higher education when wealthy Montreal merchant James McGill left a bequest that established McGill University in 1821. Bishop's College was founded by the Anglican Church in 1846 before Laval University was developed out of the Seminary of Quebec in 1852. At Laval, clergy held the prominent place, although the university offered arts, medicine, and civil law in addition to theology. While universities as a whole were mixed institutions, religious influence in them remained pronounced throughout British North America.

8.5   Social Institutions

A great diversity of voluntary institutions developed in British North America in the nineteenth century. They were often identified with particular denominations or linguistic and cultural groups, and most were divided strictly along gender lines. Male professionals in Montreal organized such associations as the St. Jean le Baptist Society (French Canadian) and the St. Patrick's Society (Irish Catholic), but the Orange Order surpassed these groups in popularity. Imported into Upper Canada from Ireland, the Orange Order transplanted Irish religious intolerance into Canada. While it claimed to be only pro-Protestant, it was essentially anti-Catholic. By 1860, the Order claimed 100 000 members in British North America. The Sons of Temperance appeared in the 1840s as part of a growing tendency towards prohibition. In Canada East, the Roman Catholic priest Charles Chiniquy preached pro-temperance addresses to large crowds about a subject that held little larger appeal in that region. In 1855 a prohibition bill was passed in New Brunswick but, following a snap election, it was rescinded before implementation.

Middle-class women were also active in voluntary organizations. While nuns in Montreal cared for the poor, the sick, and orphans, priests were involved with charitable activities through the St. Vincent de Paul societies. Wealthy English-speaking women in Montreal were particularly active in providing social services. In 1817, they organized the Female Benevolent Society to establish the Montreal General Hospital four years later. The Montreal Protestant Orphan Asylum was begun in 1822 and the Ladies' Benevolent Society started to aid destitute women after 1824.

8.5.1   The Birth of the Asylum

Voluntary organizations were unable to cope with the growing scale of problems associated with the mentally ill, criminals, or the increasing numbers of poor. Nineteenth-century society came increasingly to believe in hiding its greatest difficulties in large institutions where cures in various guises could be administered. Beginning in Toronto in 1836, Houses of Industry spread in an effort to support the poor in a more cost-effective manner than in people's own dwellings (called outdoor relief). In 1836, Saint John established the first asylum for the mentally ill in British North America, although these people had been a traditional concern of the nuns who operated general asylums in Lower Canada. Kingston Penitentiary was also intended to reform criminals when it opened in 1835. Punishment itself was seen too frequently as the cure. Orphanages were opened later to care for homeless children, and soon appeals were heard for intermediate institutions called reformatories to separate juveniles from adult criminals.

Middle-class reformers frequently viewed social problems as stemming from a lack of self-discipline and control, thus advancing the idea that many social problems were individual rather than collective in nature.

8.6 Women

The large role of women in the economy and the family stood in marked contrast to their subordination in law and politics. Women on farms performed a wide variety of tasks. Women undertook dairying, poultry raising, egg production, and vegetable gardening. Field labour was not unknown. Women also made clothes, sometimes starting with the care of sheep, the spinning of wool, weaving, and then dying, patterning, and sewing. The word "spinster" derived from farmers' daughters who remained at home and spun fibres to make thread.

While some women attempted to vote in elections early in the nineteenth century, they were prohibited from such participation by statutes in Lower Canada, Prince Edward Island, New Brunswick, and Nova Scotia. In law, married women were considered to be protected by their husbands, but in other aspects of their lives they were subordinate to their fathers—or brothers as well. Divorce was difficult and costly. Before mid-century, a special act of the legislature was required for divorce, but it could only be obtained on the grounds that her husband had committed rape or incest. Women leaving their husbands were not granted property settlements and children went to fathers except in rare cases.

By mid-century, when women began to protest, some legislative changes occurred. In 1855, a law in Canada West allowed judges to give mothers access to, or custody of, infant children when they saw fit. In 1857, Nova Scotia made it possible to obtain divorce on the grounds of adultery or desertion.

8.7 Culture

The word "culture" is elastic. In its broadest sense, the term describes a host of diverse phenomena from sports to folk beliefs and oral traditions that were associated with the majority of the population. In contrast to this popular culture, the word is also used in a more restricted sense to convey developments in the areas of art, theatre, literature, and music. While the typifications might also be termed lowbrow/highbrow, British North American output in the latter realm tended to be derivative of European models and it was produced in spare time by people with other primary occupations.

Oral traditions by which the lore of generations past was passed on were common in societies with low literacy rates. Singing and dancing provided popular entertainment, as did games such as lacrosse (learned from the Indians), cricket (developed by the British), and curling (adapted from the Scots). More formal music and theatre derived from regimental bands and garrisoned soldiers. Talented military men also provided some of the early paintings of British North Americans. By Confederation, colonial cities had created a large number of musical societies.

Indigenous literature began to develop slowly and the Maritimes was its centre in the early nineteenth century. Julia Catherine Hart (née Beckwith) of Fredericton became the first native-born novelist in 1824 when she published *St. Ursula's Convent, or The Nun of Canada*, a tale designed to appeal to Protestant prejudices. In Nova Scotia the academic Presbyterian minister, Thomas McCulloch, published not only in the areas of religion and education, but also became the founder of Canadian humor in his satirical *Stepsure* accounts that began appearing in local newspapers in 1821. McCulloch influenced Nova Scotia judge Thomas Chandler Haliburton whose literacy accomplishments were many, but who is remembered chiefly for *The Clockmaker; or The Sayings and Doings of Sam Slick, of Slickville* (1836). The Sam Slick sketches portrayed a cocksure Yankee clockmaker who surveyed the Nova Scotia scenery and hoodwinked its gullible local residents.

The Canadas evolved differing literary traditions. In Upper Canada the writings of Susanna Moodie and of her sister, Catharine Parr Traill, were emigrant literature intended for British consumption. John Richardson's novel, *Wacousta* (1832), portrayed the confrontation with the continent's expansive natural and human resources. In Canada East, a golden age of literature developed in reaction to Lord Durham's derogatory remarks about French Canadian culture. The writing of a monumental history of French Canada by François-Xavier Garneau during the 1840s served to spur a larger literary output that included novels and poetry. Much upper-class culture reflected European standards.

CHAPTER 9

Confederation

9.1 Political Instability in the Canadas

While a larger union or federation of the British North American colonies had been discussed intermittently since the time of the Constitutional Act, only the convergence of external pressures and internal problems created the movement towards Confederation in the years between 1864 and 1867. The Civil War in the United States and the American decision in 1865 to end the Reciprocity Treaty fostered military and economic uncertainty. At the same time, Britain wanted the colonies to assume a greater measure of responsibility for their own defence. Yet the determining factors that led to Confederation were political instability in the Canadas and a desire in the Maritimes for larger markets for their products. No constituent assembly was called to write the new constitution nor was a referendum or plebiscite held. Confederation was as unpopular in some quarters as it was vaunted in others.

During the 1850s political life in the Union of the Canadas became increasingly unstable. As the two regions were so large and different, it was necessary to have two solicitors general, one for the Common Law tradition of Canada West and the other for Canada East's Civil Law. There were also separate educational systems. Not even the capital could be agreed upon. At first the Union legislators met in Kingston and then in Montreal up to 1849, but afterwards they alternated between Quebec City and Toronto. The question of a permanent capital became so divisive that the matter was referred to Queen Victoria who chose Bytown (Ottawa) on the Ottawa River.

The emergence of the double majority principle showed that the two colonies were in difficulty. According to this view—albeit never legislated—ministries needed to have majorities in both of the Union's sections. Furthermore, it was argued that legislation affecting only one section needed majority support of the members from that region to become law. While this made it difficult to form governments, part of the political problem also lay in the greater strength of the Clear Grits in Canada West than the Rouges in Canada East.

The political instability that resulted from these developments was best illustrated in the double shuffle of 1858. After the Liberal Conservative ministry of John A. Macdonald and George-Etienne Cartier was defeated, the government resigned. Due to the strength of the Clear Grits in the Assembly, the Governor General called on George Brown and Antoine-Aimé Dorion to form a new ministry. According to constitutional practices of the time, ministers in a new government had to resign their seats and stand in by-elections. Weakened thus, the Brown-Dorion government also went down to defeat and the Governor General called Macdonald back. This time the need for by-elections was avoided by the previous ministers assuming only new portfolios. E.P. Taché became the figurehead leader of the new ministry, but its real force remained Macdonald and Cartier. Thus, three governments had been formed in a single year and there had been no essential change! Again, between 1861 and 1864 there were two elections and three administrations without either side being able to command a majority.

9.2 Anglo-American Entanglements

Although Britain had declared neutrality in the American Civil War, her trade with the southern Confederacy had antagonized many Northerners. The ships constructed in Britain for the southern states, of which the *Alabama* was the best known, led some Northerners to demand war reparations. Further, in 1861, ships of the Northern navy stopped the British steamer *Trent* and forcibly removed two Confederate ambassadors. In response to this hostile action, Britain sent 14 000 troops to strengthen her British North American garrisons. Tensions also erupted in 1864 after some Confederate sympathizers terrorized St. Alban's in Vermont and then sought refuge across the border. When they were arrested in Canada East but let off on a legal technicality, Northern tempers flared. At the end of the Civil War, some extremists argued that the Northern army should be used to annex the British North American colonies to the United States. The American government resolved not to renew the Reciprocity Treaty, which was to lapse in 1866.

At the conclusion of the Civil War, Britain decided to withdraw its land forces from the continent and turn over defence to the colonies themselves. Because a larger colonial union would be better able to manage military affairs, the Colonial Office in London would actively support the movement towards Confederation in Canada.

9.3   Maritime Union

Ideas about a larger union of the Maritime colonies had been around for many decades but without being resolved. Frustrated when plans for the projected Intercolonial Railway failed to materialize, some politicians advocated closer cooperation to promote larger markets and the development of economic infrastructure. By 1867 Nova Scotia had managed to build only 235 kilometres of railway; but the cost of $7.5 million had added to the colony's growing public debt. As New Brunswick had also acquired a large public debt for railroads, Premier Charles Tilley found that he could not push forward the Intercolonial or other railways. Newfoundland's slumping economy caused some politicians to consider a union of the Atlantic colonies, but many continued to see its affairs as separate from those of the continent.

9.4   The West

Until the late 1850s, Easterners had considered the Prairies largely as a "desert" unfit for settlement. Missionaries tended to confirm these views. Two scientific expeditions in 1857, one British and the other Canadian, changed the minds of many people on this subject when they issued their reports. British Captain John Palliser agreed with University of Toronto geology professor Henry Youle Hind that much of the southern Prairies could be cultivated. These reports fuelled the cause of those like George Brown and the Clear Grits who championed the acquisition of Rupert's Land from the Hudson's Bay Company to compensate for Canada West's dwindling reserves of arable lands.

9.5   The Great Coalition

To George Brown, the best hope for overcoming the political deadlock in the Canadas lay in a larger federal union. Following further political difficulties in 1864, Brown entered into negotiations with his adversary John A. Macdonald about forming a coalition Cabinet to include Taché and Cartier. Brown's conditions were that the new government commit itself to "rep-by-pop," that it work towards a larger federation of the British North American colonies, and that the Northwest be incorporated into this Confederation. In the "Great Coalition" of 1864, Brown and two other Reformers entered the government, which already represented the Liberal Conservatives of Canada East and West. The only major political party excluded was the Rouges of Canada East. The new government secured an invitation to discuss a federation at a meeting of Maritime governments in Charlottetown.

9.6   The Charlottetown and Quebec Conferences

At Charlottetown in 1864, the principal intention of the Canadians was to interest Nova Scotia, New Brunswick, and Prince Edward Island in a larger federation. Their proposals included continued loyalty to the Crown, a strong central government within a federal union (in which the provinces would control local affairs), and a federal representation in an upper house based on regions and in the lower house based on population. These ideas were sufficiently attractive and another conference was called at Quebec City later in the year. Newfoundland, which had not sent delegates to Charlottetown, dispatched representatives to Quebec.

The essentials of the Confederation agreement were hammered out at the Quebec Conference and embodied in 72 resolutions. The degree of centralization in the new Confederation became the main issue. John A. Macdonald favoured a legislative union and viewed the future provinces as little more than municipal governments— because he believed that overly powerful state governments had led to the Civil War. But not all agreed with his ideas. The Maritimes feared the loss of their identity in a union, and French Canadians wanted provisions that would protect their distinctness.

Many compromises were reached at Quebec, but they contributed to the creation of a strong central government. Representation in the upper house (Senate) was to be based on 24 seats given to each of the Canadas and the Maritimes—with Newfoundland and the West being offered four seats each. Senate appointments were to be for life. In the projected House of Commons, representation by population prevailed. While bicameralism (or a two house system) allowed delegates to address both regional and democratic concerns, the federal government was given the most important powers in the areas of defence, foreign affairs, currency, banking, international and interprovincial trade, criminal law, Indian affairs, and interprovincial transportation. While the provinces were accorded the areas of education, municipal administration, natural resources, public lands, and commerce within their borders, immigration and agriculture were to be shared jointly. The denominational school system of Canada West was guaranteed and the new federal government was to build the Intercolonial Railway.

Most importantly, the federal government could levy any taxes, but the provinces were limited to direct taxes only. The new federation would assume the debts of the individual colonies, and subsidies would be paid to the provinces to compensate for reduced revenue. The central government was also given residual powers over areas not specified—empowered to disallow provincial legislation, and given responsibility for appointing lieutenant-governors in the provinces. The federal government was to legislate for "the peace, order, and good government" of the new country.

9.7 The Debates Over Confederation

Since the legislatures of each colony were to pass individual resolutions regarding Confederation, the focus after the Quebec Conference shifted to the colonial capitals.

Confederation was debated in the legislature but no election was called on the issue nor was a referendum held. The Rouges were the principal opponents. They objected to the centralist features of the proposals, calling them more a legislative union than a federation. They also dissented from undemocratic features, such as having Senators appointed for life terms. The Rouges feared that French Canada would be marginalized in a larger country, and they wanted a plebiscite held. George-Etienne Cartier responded that the French language would be protected because bilingualism was required in the federal Parliament and Quebec Assembly, as well as in the federal courts and the judiciary of the new province of Quebec. Provinces were also accorded responsibility over civil law, religion, and education. Cartier forecast a new "political nationality" that would not challenge the "cultural nationality" of French Canada. When the votes were cast, members from Canada West approved the Confederation scheme wholeheartedly, but among members from Canada East it passed with only a slim majority.

Only in New Brunswick was Confederation put to popular test through an election in 1865. The anti-Confederation forces scored a stunning victory. The British government then ordered Lieutenant-Governor Arthur Gordon to work actively in support of Confederation. When a new election was called in 1866 following the resignation of the anti-Confederation government, the government of the Canadas gave financial support to those favouring Confederation.

A raid into New Brunswick by members of the Fenian Brotherhood strengthened the hands of those in favour of Confederation. The Fenians were an Irish-American group hoping to get Britain to favour home rule in Ireland by pressuring British North America. A second and larger Fenian raid across the Niagara River into Canada West was repulsed, but it too raised the need for greater military security. Tilley's forces won the election and carried New Brunswick into Confederation.

While the pro-Confederation forces in Nova Scotia were headed by Premier Charles Tupper, Joseph Howe led the opposition to the scheme. Howe emphasized the lack of ties between Nova Scotia and the Canadas, noting that Nova Scotia looked instead towards the Atlantic and Britain. Like Dorion, he wanted the people consulted in a plebiscite. In both New Brunswick and Nova Scotia, business people were concerned that the new federal government's control of tariffs might remove their protection and flood their markets with goods from the united Province of Canada. In the end, the anti-

Confederation forces were so strong in Nova Scotia that Charles Tupper's resolution in the legislature made no reference to the plan itself. As the resolution simply empowered the government to continue negotiations for a British North American union, the measure passed readily.

Prince Edward Island and Newfoundland were both less readily challenged by external threats and felt less attracted to proposals such as the Intercolonial Railway. Both colonies decided not to join.

9.8   The British North America Act

Before the Confederation agreement was embodied in the British North America Act—to be presented to the British Parliament—one last conference of colonial representatives was held in 1866 in London, England. At the conference, the contentious issue of separate schools was solved by applying the Quebec clause on education to all the provinces. Section 93 of the Act specified that while provinces controlled education, they could not adversely affect the denominational character of their system. If the legally recognized school systems of religious minorities were challenged by a province, one provision allowed appeal to the governor general and another empowered the federal government to pass remedial legislation in favour of the religious minority.

While Joseph Howe tried again to influence British politicians against Confederation, they did not waver in their support. The name for the new country was also an object of debate. John A. Macdonald preferred "Kingdom of Canada" to emphasize separateness from Britain, but in the end Biblical references prevailed. Leonard Tilley chanced upon Psalm 72:

> Let his dominion also be from sea to sea,
> and from river unto the world's end
> And blessed be the name of his majesty for ever.

These lines provided the name "Dominion of Canada" and the country's motto, "from sea to sea."

Passed by the British Parliament and dated July 1, 1867, the British North America Act provided Canada with a written constitu-